PAUL & JESUS

PAUL&JESUS

F.F. BRUCE

WIPF & STOCK · Eugene, Oregon

Wipf and Stock Publishers
199 W 8th Ave, Suite 3
Eugene, OR 97401

Paul and Jesus
By Bruce, F. F.
Copyright©1974 Baker Publishing
ISBN 13: 978-1-5326-9012-9
Publication date 4/26/2019
Previously published by Baker Book House, 1974

TO
CHARLES AND ELVA GREY

ONTARIO BIBLE COLLEGE'S
ELMORE HARRIS SERIES
OF EVANGELICAL BOOKS

God and Evil
by William Fitch

Encounter in the Non-Christian Era
by John W. Sanderson, Jr.

*The Old Testament
in Contemporary Preaching*
by Walter C. Kaiser, Jr.

Paul and Jesus
by F. F. Bruce

Contents

Foreword

These chapters from the pen ʋf the outstanding New Testament scholar Dr. F. F. Bruce form more than just another "evangelical treatise."

They consist of strong, scriptural, and well-researched material on Paul as the mouthpiece of God; the protagonist of the Lord Jesus Christ; the most able Christian theologian the church has known.

Dr. Bruce believes firmly in the unity of Paul's and Jesus' teachings. He finds no justification of "Pauline ideas"; no warping or twisting of the truth in Paul's epistles; no obstruction in the free flow of spiritual understanding from Matthew to Timothy—indeed from ʼMatthew to Revelation, since all these men wrote as they were directed by the Holy Spirit (II Peter 1:21).

The critic who reads these pages will be left abashed, silenced by relentless logic and impeccable research. The believer will read with warm appreciation and firmer faith.

The church will be richer for this fine declaration of "the faith, once and for all delivered to the saints" (Jude 3) and to Paul, who felt he was the least of them.

We are grateful to Dr. Bruce for yet another volume to enrich and deepen our understanding of God's Word.

DOUGLAS C. PERCY
Ontario Bible College

11

Preface

This little book contains a revised version of the six lectures delivered at Ontario Bible College's annual Thomas F. Staley Academic Lecture Series.

The work of preparing them for publication recalls to memory several happy days spent in Toronto in the company of the faculty, students, and friends of Ontario Bible College. It is at once a duty and a pleasure to make special mention of the kindness of the Rev. E. L. Simmonds, chairman of the department of biblical studies. It was from him that the initial invitation came, and I think with gratitude of his thoughtful planning of my schedule and provision for my leisure hours.

My indebtedness to Miss Margaret Hogg is increased by her careful typing of this further work.

September, 1973   F. F. B.

Introduction

In his recent book, *Reapproaching Paul,* Dr. Morton Scott Enslin begins with the remark that "a half-century ago it was the fashion to write books entitled 'Jesus and Paul' or 'Jesus or Paul.' In consequence, the popular pictures of the two central heroes, both unique in Christian history and affection, stood clear: Jesus was the founder, establisher, of the resultant Christian church for which He had lived and died; Paul was in a real sense its second founder and its greatest theologian. In the eyes of some there was regret that this latter fact was the case, for to them Paul, influential though he had become, was really a liability. It was he , they were sure, who had muddied the clear waters; and in consequence there was a current, or at least an undercurrent, of desire which may be styled 'Back to Jesus' and which virtually meant 'Away from Paul.'

"Today [Dr. Enslin continues] there is a bit more restraint toward both of these characters. Jesus lived and died a Jew, with his eye fixed on the new age promised to Abraham and long awaited by Abraham's children. Paul, too, was a Jew and remained such throughout his stormy life. He had been converted, but not from Judaism to Christianity—for there was no such thing in his day—but to what he was convinced was the true Judaism, an unqualified obedience to, and deathless love for,

15

God's greatest gift to man, Jesus Christ, the complete and final revelation of himself and his will for men."[1]

The movement "away from Paul" has not come to a full halt, whether or not it can be described as a movement "back to Jesus." The Paul of popular prejudice and the Jesus of popular prejudice are both figments of the imagination, so that a movement away from the one may well be a movement towards the other; but if we are concerned with the real Paul and the real Jesus, then a movement away from Paul turns out to be at the same time a movement away from Jesus, who found no more faithful interpreter than Paul.

So far as popular prejudice goes, Paul regularly has a bad press. In *The Times Literary Supplement of London* for November 26, 1971, two books were reviewed together—*The Occult* by Colin Wilson and *The Devil and All His Works* by Dennis Wheatley. According to the anonymous reviewer, Wilson thinks that Jesus was a "nice visionary" but maintains that "it is arguable that St. Paul's 'crosstianity' was one of the greatest disasters that has ever befallen the human race: a great black shadow of intolerance, a super totalitarianism that makes communism seem harmless by comparison"; while Wheatley for his part calls Paul "an intolerant religious bigot" who "demanded obedience with threats of Hellfire."[2] (Against cast-iron prejudice like this, what would be the use of pointing out that Paul never mentions hell once from one end to the other of his extant writings?)

Reading this sort of stuff makes one rub one's eyes in perplexity. Where has this picture of Paul come from? The authentic Paul is Paul the preacher of emancipation, Paul who announced the replacement of the yoke of legal bondage by the freedom of the Spirit, Paul who proclaimed that men had come of age in Christ and refused to let religion be treated any more as a matter of rules and regulations such as befitted the apron-string stage of their spiritual development, Paul whose insistence that in Christ there is neither male nor female entitles him to be recognized as the patron-saint of women's liberation, Paul the author of that great hymn in praise of love, Paul whose "genius for friendship" has become a proverb—almost a cliché.

There are, of course, differences between Jesus and Paul. Jesus was Lord; Paul was His servant. On the plane of human experience, Jesus and Paul, while both Jews, differed in birth and upbringing, in education, in environment, in temperament,

1. (Philadelphia, 1972), p. 11.
2. p. 1471.

in idiom. As for temperament, Paul may beseech his friends by "the meekness and gentleness of Christ" (II Cor. 10:1); but these were not qualities which came to Paul naturally. As for idiom, we can readily distinguish between Jesus' parabolic style with its telling pictures drawn from daily life and Paul's strength in point-by-point argument of the Hellenistic *diatribé* pattern.

But they both shocked the guardians of Israel's law by their refusal to let godly people seek security before God in their own righteousness; they both made mortal enemies of the chief-priestly establishment in Jerusalem; they were both executed by the sentence of Roman courts. And more important still, Paul saw more clearly than most into the inwardness of Jesus' teaching as, following His example, he proclaimed a message of good news for the outsider.

1

"Christ after the Flesh"

Paul is our earliest literary authority for the historical Jesus. True, he does not tell us much about the historical Jesus, in comparison with what we can learn from the Evangelists, but he does tell us a little more than that Jesus was born and died. Jesus was an Israelite, he says, descended from Abraham (Gal. 3:16) and David (Rom. 1:3); who lived under the Jewish law (Gal. 4:4); who was betrayed, and on the night of his betrayal instituted a memorial meal of bread and wine (I Cor. 11:23ff.); who endured the Roman penalty of crucifixion (I Cor. 1:23; Gal. 3:1, 13; 6:14, etc.), although Jewish authorities were somehow involved in His death (I Thess. 2:15); who was buried, rose the third day and was thereafter seen alive by many eyewitnesses on various occasions, including one occasion on which He was so seen by over five hundred at once, of whom the majority were alive twenty-five years later (I Cor. 15:4ff.). In this summary of the evidence for the reality of Christ's resurrection, Paul shows a sound instinct for the necessity of marshalling personal testimony in support of what might well appear an incredible assertion.

Paul knows of the Lord's apostles, of whom Peter and John are mentioned by name as "pillars" of the Jerusalem community (Gal. 2:9), and of His brothers, of whom James is similarly mentioned (Gal. 1:19; 2:9). He knows that the Lord's brothers and apostles, including Peter, were married (I Cor. 9:5), an incidental agreement with the Gospel story of the healing of Peter's mother-in-law (Mark 1:30). He quotes sayings of Jesus on occasion, e.g., His teaching on marriage and divorce (I Cor. 7:10f.) and on the right of gospel preachers to have their material needs supplied (I Cor. 9:14); and the words He used at the institution of the Lord's Supper (I Cor. 11:24ff.).

Even where he does not quote the actual sayings of Jesus, he shows throughout his works how well acquainted he was with them. In particular, we ought to compare the ethical section of the Epistle to the Romans (12:1—15:7), where Paul summarizes the practical implications of the gospel for the lives of believers, with the Sermon on the Mount, to see how thoroughly imbued the apostle was with the teaching of his Master. Besides, there and elsewhere Paul's chief argument in his ethical instruction is the example of Christ Himself. And the character of Christ as understood by Paul is in perfect agreement with His character as portrayed in the Gospels. When Paul speaks of "the meekness and gentleness of Christ" (II Cor. 10:1), we remember our Lord's own words, "I am meek and lowly in heart" (Matt. 11:29). The self-denying Christ of the Gospels is the one of whom Paul says, "Christ did not please himself" (Rom. 15:3); and just as the Christ of the Gospels called on His followers to deny themselves (Mark 8:34), so the apostle insists that, after the example of Christ, it is our Christian duty "to bear the infirmities of the weak, and not to please ourselves" (Rom. 15:1). He who said: "I am among you as the servant" (Luke 22:27), and performed the menial task of washing His disciples' feet (John 13:4ff.), is He who, according to Paul, "took the form of a slave" (Phil. 2:7).

In short, the outline of the gospel story insofar as we can trace it in the writings of Paul agrees with the outline which we find elsewhere in the New Testament, and in the four Gospels in particular. Paul himself is at pains to point out that the gospel which he preached was basically one and the same as that preached by the other apostles (I Cor. 15:11), a striking claim if we consider that Paul was neither a companion of the earthly Jesus nor of the original apostles, and that he vigorously asserts his complete independence of these latter.

Even so, from the Pauline letters we should not know that Jesus habitually taught in parables, that He healed the sick or performed other messianic "signs"; we should not know of His baptism and temptation, of His Galilean ministry, of the confession at Caesarea Philippi or of the transfiguration which followed a week later; and although we have clear and repeated references to His crucifixion, we should know nothing of the events which precipitated it.

The Change of Perspective in History

"The appointed time has fully come," said Jesus as He inaugurated His Galilean ministry, "and the kingdom of God has drawn near; repent and believe in the good news" (Mark 1:14f.). "When the time had fully come," wrote Paul to the Galatians, "God set forth his Son . . . so that we might receive adoption as sons" (Gal. 4:4f.). The substance of both proclamations is the same, but there is a change of perspective; the original Preacher has become the Preached One, for Good Friday and Easter have intervened. In Jesus' message and Paul's we have to distinguish not so much two different types of faith (as Martin Buber had it)[1] as two different *ages* of faith.

The *form* of Jesus' Galilean preaching, with its echoes of Old Testament prophecy and apocalyptic, would have been as unintelligible to the pagans of Corinth as the *form* of Paul's preaching in Corinth would have been two decades earlier to the Galileans. But between the *essence* of Paul's preaching and the *essence* of Jesus' preaching there is no such gulf, given the time-shift between the two.

"Paul," wrote Albert Schweitzer, "shares with Jesus the eschatological world-view and the eschatological expectation, with all that these imply. The only difference is the hour in the world-clock in the two cases. To use another figure, both are looking towards the same mountain range, but whereas Jesus sees it as lying before Him, Paul already stands upon it and its first slopes are already behind him."[2] Without some such appreciation of the eschatological factor, it will be difficult to discern the true relationship between Jesus and Paul.

In the ministry of Jesus, the kingdom of God with the fulfillment of His promises of blessing for mankind is in process of inauguration. The kingdom of God arrived with Jesus' ministry, but its powers were not unleashed in their fullness. Until He underwent the "baptism" of His passion, He was conscious of restraint (Luke 12:50). But with the passion and triumph of the Son of Man the restraint would be removed and, as He told

---

1. Cf. *Two Types of Faith* (London, 1951), pp. 44ff.
2. *The Mysticism of Paul the Apostle* (London, 1931), p. 113.

His hearers on one occasion, some of them would witness the
advent of the kingdom of God "with power" in their present
lifetime (Mark 9:1).

For Paul the kingdom's advent with power has taken place.
Jesus has been "designated Son of God in power according to
the Spirit of holiness by his resurrection from the dead" (Rom.
1:4). The power which God exerted in raising Jesus from the
dead is now at work in the followers of Jesus, conveyed to them
by His indwelling Spirit; by that same indwelling Spirit the
love of God, demonstrated supremely in the self-giving death
of Christ for His people's sins, is poured out in their hearts. The
perspective has inevitably changed, because the death and resurrection of Jesus, which were future events during His earthly
ministry, are now past events, or rather parts of one compre-
hensive saving event, by which the irresistible advance of the
cause of God has been released in the world. The kingdom has
thereby been inaugurated; what remains to be done before its
consummation has mainly the nature of mopping-up operations
after the decisive victory which has already been won. Hostile
spiritual forces, already disabled, have to be destroyed; with the
destruction of death, the last of these forces, the resurrection
age will be consummated, although its blessings are enjoyed
here and now through the Spirit by those who have experienced
faith-union with Christ. For them the age to come has dawned,
although for others it may still be future. "Therefore, if any one
is in Christ, he is a new creation; the old has passed away, be-
hold, the new has come" (II Cor. 5:17).

The Change of Perspective in Experience

The change of perspective of which we are aware as we move
from Jesus to Paul is, then, a change for which the words of
Jesus have prepared us. Absolutely, it is a change which can be
dated in terms of world history, around A.D. 30; empirically, it
is a change which takes place whenever a man or woman comes
to be "in Christ," as had happened to Paul himself. And when
the change takes place thus empirically, it revolutionizes one's
whole outlook. "From now on, therefore, we regard no one
from a human point of view; even though we once regarded
Christ from a human point of view, we regard him thus no
longer" (II Cor. 5:16).

These words of II Corinthians 5:16 have played a crucial part
in much discussion of Paul's relation and attitude to Jesus. What

is meant by regarding Christ "from a human point of view"—
"after the flesh," as *kata sarka* is literally rendered by our older
versions? (Of course, if Walter Schmithals is right in marking
these words as a gnostic gloss, we need pay no further attention
to them; but he is not.)[3]

One interpretation of the words, not so commonly expressed
today as in earlier generations, takes them to mean "that Paul
had known Christ as men know one another, that is, had seen
Him with his eyes." So Johannes Weiss put it, and he went on:
"Indeed, the expression implies more than this; it signifies the
impression made not only by outward appearance, but by
personality, the impression received by direct personal acquaintance."[4] He concluded that Paul had most probably seen and
heard Jesus in Jerusalem during Holy Week, and that it is this
kind of "knowledge" that Paul is now disparaging in comparison
with the new knowledge of Him that he has "according to the
Spirit."

Whether Paul ever did see or hear Jesus before the crucifixion
is not in question here. Perhaps he did; if W. C. van Unnik's
thesis[5] be accepted, that Jerusalem was the city of Paul's boy-
hood and upbringing, as well as of his higher education at the
feet of Gamaliel, it is quite probable that he did. But that there
is any reference to such seeing or hearing in II Corinthians 5:16
is extremely doubtful. It is hardly going too far to say with R.
Bultmann: "that he [Paul] even saw Jesus and was impressed
by him is . . . to be read out of II Cor. 5:16 only by fantasy."[6]
On the other hand, Professor Bultmann's own interpretation of
this text can be read out of it only if it first be read into it. For
him, the knowledge of Christ "after the flesh" which Paul de-
preciates is much the same thing as an interest in "the Jesus of
history." It is, he says, "illegitimate to go behind the kerygma,
using it as a 'source,' in order to reconstruct a 'historical Jesus'
with his 'messianic consciousness,' his 'inner life,' or his
'heroism.' That would be merely 'Christ after the flesh,' who
is no longer. It is not the historical Jesus, but Jesus Christ, the
Christ preached, who is the Lord."[7]

Bultmann feels that an appeal to history may on the one
hand seem to preserve something of man's autonomy over

3. *Gnosticism in Corinth* (Nashville, 1971), pp. 302ff.
4. *Paul and Jesus* (London, 1909), pp. 47f.
5. *Tarsus or Jerusalem?* (London, 1962).
6. *Existence and Faith* (1964), p. 133.
7. *Faith and Understanding,* i (London, 1966), p. 241.

against God in Christ, and on the other hand make the basis of faith something which is liable to change in the course of historical study. Indeed, his historical skepticism with regard to the life of Jesus and the gospel story is probably bound up with his insistence that the only Christ who matters for faith is the Christ with whose challenge man is confronted in the kerygma. But if the Christ of the kerygma is not also the Jesus of history, there is the danger that our faith may be placed in "cunningly devised fables." The Christian with a historical conscience can and should ask historical questions about the One whom he has believed. When Emil Brunner in one of his earlier works says (in similar vein to Bultmann) that "Jesus of Nazareth, the rabbi, the so-called historical Jesus, was an object of no interest for the early Christians and it is of no interest today for those who have preserved some understanding of what Christian faith means,"[8] his statement must be denied in both its parts.

We can understand the point that Brunner and Bultmann are making; we can see that they are overstating something that is valid, but it is not the point that Paul makes. Still less is Paul concerned to disparage the knowledge of Jesus enjoyed by the twelve by virtue of their companionship with Him during His ministry in comparison with his own present knowledge of Jesus in the Spirit, as has also been suggested. Whatever differences there might be between him and the twelve, they, like him, were "in Christ"; they, like him, possessed the Spirit, as Paul himself would be the first to assert. The contrast which Paul is making is one between his former attitude to Christ (as to the world in general) and his present attitude to Christ (as to the world in general) now that he is "in Christ." The point is brought out excellently by the New English Bible: "With us therefore worldly standards have ceased to count in our estimate of any man; even if once they counted in our understanding of Christ, they do so now no longer." When Paul speaks of the possibility that he may "have known Christ after the flesh," "after the flesh" is not an adjectival phrase qualifying the noun "Christ"; it is an adverbial phrase modifying the verb "have known."

Even so, the precise meaning of these words demands further attention: when Paul speaks of his former knowledge of Christ after the flesh, is he referring to his former conception of the Messiah, which has been radically altered now that he has come to recognize the Messiah in Jesus; or is he referring to his

---

8. *The Word and the World* (London, 1931), pp. 87f.

former hostility to Jesus and His followers, which has now been replaced by apostolic devotion to Jesus and brotherly love to His followers?

In either case, now that, for Paul, Jesus and the Messiah are identical, the distinction, otherwise important, loses its practical relevance. More probably, Paul means that his former conception of the Messiah was "worldly" and wrong. If so, nothing can be farther from the mark than the conclusion reached by William Wrede in his study of Paul (1907). He dissented radically from the affirmations of Wellhausen, Harnack, and other contemporaries of his who maintained that Paul was the man who most truly understood the gospel of Christ. Far from it, in Wrede's view: Paul had no interest in the historical Jesus and His authentic message, but remodelled them completely to the shape of his own antecedent conception of the Messiah, a conception shared in part with apocalyptic pictures of an elect being who resides in heaven before he comes to earth.

How otherwise, he asked, could the "enormous gulf" between the "historical human personality" of Jesus and the "supramundane, divine being" whom Paul called the Lord Jesus Christ be accounted for? *"The picture of Christ did not originate in an impression of the personality of Jesus"*—an impression which Paul "certainly never received." On the contrary, the picture was in Paul's mind already: *"Paul believed in such a celestial being, in a divine Christ, before he believed in Jesus."* Then, "in the moment of conversion, when Jesus appeared before him in the shining glory of his risen existence, Paul identified him with his own Christ, and straightway transferred to Jesus all the conceptions which he already had of the celestial being."[9]

The truth of the matter, in fact, is exactly the other way round. Once the glorified Jesus appeared in him, and he learned that Jesus is Lord, it was no longer a question of adapting Jesus to his previous conception of the Christ: "the Christ," says Paul in other words, "is not the figure I formerly imagined Him to be; the true Christ is the crucified Jesus, risen from the dead and glorified. As for the Christ of my former 'worldly' imagination, henceforth I know *that* Christ no more."

Of course, if Jesus was the Christ, Paul's whole attitude to Jesus, as well as his conception of the Messiah, was revolutionized. Once upon a time, as he said to the younger Agrippa, he thought it his duty "to do many things in opposing the name of

---

9. W. Wrede, *Paul* (London, 1907), p. 151.

Jesus of Nazareth" (Acts 26:9); now that his eyes were enlightened, he knew it was his duty "to bring about the obedience of faith . . . among all the nations" for the sake of that very name (Rom. 1:5). What God had wrought in the saving act of Christ became effective by the Spirit a few years later in Paul's life when the risen Christ appeared to him and changed his entire perspective. To this resurrection appearance he appealed in confirmation of his claim to be an apostle (I Cor. 9:1); to it, as the occasion when it pleased God to reveal His Son to him, he traced his call and empowerment to be Christ's ambassador among the Gentiles (Gal. 1:15f.); to it he traced the impartation to him by the risen Christ of the very gospel which he was commissioned to proclaim.

2

Paul's Gospel as Revelation

In what is one of his earliest extant letters, if not (as I believe) the earliest of them all—the Letter to the Galatians—Paul says: "I would have you know, my brothers, that the gospel which was preached by me is not man's gospel. For I did not receive it from man, nor was I taught it, but it came through a revelation of Jesus Christ" (1:11f.). In the phrase "a revelation of Jesus Christ" the genitive "of Jesus Christ" is probably objective —i.e., it was Jesus Christ who was revealed—in the light of verses 15f., where Paul tells how "he who had set me apart before I was born, and had called me through his grace, was pleased to reveal his Son to me,[1] in order that I might preach him among the Gentiles." The revelation of Jesus Christ coincided with Paul's conversion, when he both received his gospel and the commission to proclaim it among the Gentiles.

Our interpretation of these words must take into account other statements by Paul in which he implies that some aspects of his message were "received" by him from those who were "in Christ" before him, and affirms plainly that they were shared by those others. We shall look at those statements later, but the fact of their presence alongside such a forthright declaration

---

1. Gk. *en emoi* probably combines the two senses "to me" (RSV) and "in me" (KJV).

27

as that in Galatians 1:11f. reminds us that there is a dialectic in Paul's thinking which must not be ignored. It will not do to concentrate on one side of the dialectic only as though it represented the whole Paul, or at least the true Paul.

Professor Bultmann sums up the side represented in Galatians 1:11f. when he says of Paul:

> After his conversion he made no effort toward contact with Jesus' disciples or the Jerusalem Church for instruction concerning Jesus and His ministry. On the contrary, he vehemently protests his independence from them in Gal. 1-2.[2]

This is true so far as it goes, but only so far as it goes. It does not take account of the fact that within three years, if not immediately, Paul did make contact with Jesus' disciples, as he himself goes on to say in Galatians 1:18f. To this we shall return, but for the moment we must consider what we should understand by the gospel which Paul received by way of revelation. We shall probably be right in saying that to Paul the revelation of the gospel was bound up with the revelation of the Son of God; it might be summed up in the statement: "Jesus is the risen Lord." Others may have made this their confession and proclamation before Paul did, and he was no doubt aware of this; but it was not from them that he received it. On the contrary, when he heard such language on their lips, it seemed utter blasphemy to him. How could One who died under the curse of God—the curse pronounced in Deuteronomy 21:23 on "a hanged man"—be the risen Lord, the elect of God, the Son of the Most High, as those disciples brazenly affirmed? No; the one thing that could have convinced Paul that Jesus was the risen Lord was his Damascus-road experience; this henceforth was the essence of his gospel, and he owed it directly to that "revelation of Jesus Christ." The historical data of the life and ministry of Jesus, whether he knew them previously or learned them subsequently, were subordinate to this; it was to this that they owed all their significance.

In keeping with what we can infer from Paul's own testimony is the statement in Acts 9:20 that, after his conversion and baptism at Damascus, "in the synagogues immediately he proclaimed Jesus, saying, 'He is the Son of God.' "[3] How had he

---

2. *Theology of the New Testament,* i (London, 1952), p. 188.

3. It might be objected that "in the synagogues" he would have little opportunity to preach Christ "among the Gentiles." But it may be that in Damascus as elsewhere there were Gentile God-fearers who attended the synagogues.

come to believe that Jesus was the Son of God? Because, in his own words, God "was pleased to reveal his Son to me" (Gal. 1:16).

If revelation was the act of God, seeing was the reaction of Paul. "Have I not seen Jesus our Lord?" is his indignant rhetorical question in reply to some who queried his apostolic status (I Cor. 9:1). Or, using the passive voice of the verb "to see," he adds his personal testimony to the list of other witnesses to the risen Christ in I Corinthians 15:8: "Last of all . . . he *appeared* also to me."[4]

The revelational aspect of Paul's gospel is closely bound up with that understanding of Christian existence expressed in his distinctive phrase: "in Christ." This is certainly an understanding of Christianity which came to Paul not by tradition through others, but by direct revelation, and initially by the words "why are you persecuting me?" addressed to him by the risen Lord (Acts 9:4; 22:7; 26:14).

Again, when Paul thinks of the gospel as something conveyed to him by revelation, he sometimes describes it as a "mystery," a word which he applies now to the gospel as a whole and now to some particular aspect of it. We must bear in mind that the word *mystery* in its distinctive biblical usage denotes some phase of the divine purpose, especially with reference to the "latter days," formerly concealed but now disclosed—disclosed by special revelation.

The Mystery of the Gospel

In what appears to be, on balance, the true reading of I Corinthians 2:1, Paul refers to the gospel which he brought to Corinth as "the mystery of God."[5] This "mystery" is summed up in "Jesus Christ and him crucified." It was imparted to the Corinthians in plain, unrhetorical but nevertheless effective language, which produced conviction and led to their salvation. Later, however—perhaps when they had listened to the eloquence and ingenuity of Apollos' expository preaching—some of them began to feel that Paul's message was elementary, and they wondered whether his failure to give them more "advanced" teaching was due to unwillingness or inability on his part. He

---

4. See pp. 53f.
5. B and the majority of later witnesses read "the testimony (*martyrion*) of God" instead of "the mystery (*mysterion*) of God," which is found in P46 and the first hand in Aleph.

assures them that any inability lies in them and not in himself; they are not mature enough to assimilate the wisdom which he could impart to those who were spiritually full grown. This wisdom he calls "God's wisdom in a mystery," the hidden wisdom decreed before the ages for His people's glorification. But it is evident that this "wisdom in a mystery" is not something additional to the saving message of Christ crucified; it is in Christ crucified, he has just told them (1:23f.), that divine wisdom is embodied. It consists rather in the more detailed unfolding of the divine wisdom which is summed up in Christ crucified—and if we seek for that more detailed unfolding, perhaps we shall find it in the letter to the Ephesians.

Similarly in the doxology appended to the letter to the Romans, Paul's gospel, the preaching of Jesus Christ, is equated with "the revelation (*apokalypsis*) of the mystery which was kept secret for long ages but is now disclosed and through the prophetic writings is made known to all nations" (16:25f.).

This mystery cannot be distinguished from "the mystery of Christ" of which Paul speaks in Colossians 4:3. In exhorting the Colossians to prayer, he asks them to pray for himself as he awaits his appearance before Caesar, "that God may open to us a door for the word, to declare the mystery of Christ, on account of which I am in prison, that I may make it clear, as I ought to speak." That the "mystery of Christ" is the gospel entrusted to Paul is plain from the context; this is further confirmed by the parallel passage in Ephesians 6:18ff.: "Pray . . . also for me, that utterance may be given me in opening my mouth boldly to proclaim the mystery of the gospel, for which I am an ambassador in chains; that I may declare it boldly, as I ought to speak." The "mystery of Christ" is the "mystery of the gospel" because it is in Christ that God's saving purpose is revealed and accomplished.

But Christ Himself is the revelation of God; hence at an earlier point in the Letter to the Colossians Paul speaks of his concern for them and for their fellow-Christians elsewhere in the Lycus valley, "that their hearts may be encouraged as they are knit together in love, to have all the riches of assured understanding and the knowledge of God's mystery, (that is) of Christ, in whom are hid all the treasures of wisdom and knowledge" (2:1-3). Paul's immediate concern is to safeguard his friends against the subtle attractions of the "Colossian heresy." He reckons that they can be most effectively safeguarded if they realize that Christ, with whom they are all united by faith, is the embodiment of the totality of the divine wisdom—the embodiment, indeed, of "the whole fulness of deity" (Col. 2:9). Since this is so, there can be no spiritual knowledge beyond Christ, or apart from Him. There is a wide range of variant readings in the text here, and some witnesses omit the genitive "of Christ," so that Paul is made to speak of "God's mystery, in which are hid all the treasures of wisdom and knowledge." The genitive "of Christ" would then be a gloss—and a very early one, since it is attested by our oldest manuscript of the Pauline corpus—but it would be a correct gloss, since "God's mystery," as here described, cannot be other than Christ Himself. This is the mystery which Paul desires his friends to know, and to know as an indwelling presence.[6]

The Pastoral Letters preserve this use of "mystery" to denote the gospel in general—"the mystery of the faith" (I Tim. 3:9) —and Christ in particular, as in I Timothy 3:16, where the great "mystery of our religion" is summed up in Him who "was manifested in the flesh . . . taken up in glory."

The Mystery of the End-Time

At the end of his resurrection chapter (I Cor. 15), most of which is devoted to arguing that the resurrection of Christians is so completely bound up with the resurrection of Christ that the denial of the former involves the denial of the latter, while the affirmation of the latter involves the affirmation of the former, Paul introduces a new revelation with the words: "Lo! I tell you a mystery" (v. 51). The "mystery" concerns the change which the living as well as the dead must undergo at the advent of Christ in order to inherit the new order of existence in the consummated kingdom of God.

To see Paul's teaching on this subject in perspective, it is useful to go back to an earlier letter in which he had dealt with the lot of believers at the time of the advent.

About A.D. 50 Paul visited the Macedonian city of Thessalonica, where he preached the gospel and founded a church (cf. Acts 17:1-9). Circumstances beyond his control, however, forced him to leave Thessalonica before he had given his converts all the teaching he believed they required. It is clear that he taught them not only "to serve the living and true God" to whom they had turned from pagan idolatry, but also "to wait for his Son from heaven, whom he raised from the dead, Jesus

---

6. See pp. 37f.

our deliverer from the coming wrath" (I Thess. 1:9f.). Such
expectant waiting implies survival to witness the great event.
But in the weeks and months that followed Paul's departure,
some of his converts died. The death of believers before the
advent of Christ was something that the Thessalonian church
had not been prepared for, and a problem was thereby created
in their minds on which they sought enlightenment. Through
Timothy, probably, whom Paul had sent back from Athens to
visit them, they submitted their problem to Paul; in fact, they
seem to have put two questions to him:

1. At Christ's advent, what will be the lot of those believers
in Him who have died before He comes?

2. When may the advent be expected?

In answering the former question, Paul assures them that
those of their number who have died before the advent will
suffer no disadvantage when it takes place: "We who are alive,
who are left until the coming of the Lord, shall not precede
those who have fallen asleep." On the contrary, when the Lord
descends from heaven with the shout of command, the arch-
angel's voice, and the trumpet blast, those who respond to His
summons first will be the dead in Christ; when they rise at His
call, brought to life with Him who died and rose again, "then
we who are alive, who are left, shall be caught up together with
them in clouds to meet the Lord in the air" (I Thess. 4:14-18).
This assurance is conveyed to them "by the word of the Lord"—
that is, on the authority of an utterance of Jesus Himself, given
either before His death or subsequently through a prophet.[7]
It has thus the status of a revelation, although the term "mystery" is not used in this context. The language and imagery are
those associated with Old Testament theophanies of redemption
and judgment—we may think of the trumpet blast which calls
home the dispersed of Israel in Isaiah 27:13 and the clouds of
heaven on which one like a son of man is brought to the
Ancient of Days in Daniel 7:13—but what is here communicated in these terms is new and distinctively Christian. Because
Jesus died and rose again, those who die believing in Him cannot fail to rise with Him; and all His people must live forever
with Him.

As for the latter and more general question, *when* the advent
would take place, Paul does little more than repeat the words of
Jesus, that it would come unexpectedly, "like a thief in the

---

7. See pp. 69f.

night" (Matt. 24:43f.; Luke 12:39f.; cf. Rev. 16:15). The call to the people of Christ therefore is to "keep awake and be sober," since (Paul adds) "God has not destined us for wrath, but to obtain salvation through our Lord Jesus Christ" (I Thess. 5:1-9).

A few years later Paul reverts to the subject, in his reply to those members of the church of Corinth who held, as he put it, that there was "no resurrection of the dead" (I Cor. 15:12). In their eyes the reanimation of corpses, which they took the resurrection doctrine to imply, was perhaps an uncongenial Jewish superstition which Paul had not yet been able to get out of his system. If, as he himself had taught them, believers in Christ had in some sense been raised from death with Him, why should they look for any further resurrection? It is evident from Paul's argument that the men to whom it was directed had no thought of denying the resurrection of Christ: if they accepted that, he urges, they must logically accept the resurrection of His people. The resurrection of Christ was the first fruits of the general resurrection-harvest which the people of Christ would experience at His advent, when death, the last enemy, would be abolished.

For Paul, this future resurrection could only be bodily resurrection. True, the immortal resurrection body would be of a different order from the present mortal body; it would be a "spiritual" body, whereas the present body was a body animated by "soul." This language is bound up with his distinction between life "in Adam," who in Genesis 2:7 is described as "a living soul," and life "in Christ," who in resurrection has become "a life-giving spirit" (I Cor. 15:45). But in this argument Paul goes beyond the assurance he had given to the Thessalonian Christians some five years earlier. Then he declared that those who survived to the advent would enjoy no advantage over the faithful departed; now he affirms, and that on the strength of a special revelation, a "mystery" newly disclosed, that those who survive will then undergo an instantaneous transformation, so that they too will be adapted to the conditions of the resurrection age. The dead—that is to say, the dead in Christ, who alone come into Paul's purview here—will rise in bodies which are not liable to corruption, while the living will exchange mortality for immortality. To much the same effect he reminds his converts at Philippi that from heaven "we await a Savior, the Lord Jesus Christ, who will change our lowly body to be like his glorious body" (Phil. 3:20f.). Basic to his thinking through-

out is the conviction that Christ and His people are so vitally
and permanently united that they must share His triumph over
death, not only in baptismal anticipation but in bodily resurrection. But as the nature of the resurrection is unfolded in a
"mystery," so is the nature of the unity in which Christ and
His people are bound together.

The Mystery of Union in Christ

This mystery is also implicit in the revelation which Paul
received on the Damascus road, and his vocation as apostle to
the Gentiles must have brought him face to face with its implications quite early in his Christian career. If the purpose of that
revelation was that Paul should proclaim the Son of God
among the Gentiles, what place did the Gentiles have in God's
saving plan, and how was it related to the place of the Jews in
His plan?

Many Jews in the first century A.D. believed that it was their
privilege to communicate the knowledge of the true God to
Gentiles: for this belief they had prophetic authority. Israel is
described by God as "the people whom I formed for myself that
they might declare my praise" (Isa. 43:21). The large number
of Gentile God-fearers attached to synagogues throughout the
Roman Empire provides ample testimony to the efficacy of
Jewish witness in this regard.

Before long, many leaders of Jewish Christianity saw this
mission as part of their responsibility. While the apostolic activity
of Paul is exceptionally well documented, it is plain that the
gospel was carried along other roads than those which he followed and was quickly established in such centers as Alexandria
and Rome, in the first instance in the Jewish communities of
those cities, expanding thence into the Gentile environment. It
was natural that the sequence "to the Jew first and also to the
Greek" (Rom. 1:16) should be understood not only of the
presentation of the gospel but of its acceptance: first, it was
thought, the Jews must be won to acknowledge in the crucified
one their true King, and then His sovereignty would spread over
the Gentile lands. This is the perspective of James's quotation of
the Septuagint rendering of Amos 9:11f. at the Council of
Jerusalem: as David from his base in Jerusalem had extended
his dominion over surrounding nations, so the Gentile mission
from the same base would lead the "residue of men" to seek

the Lord and be enrolled among the nations called by the name of the God of Israel (Acts 15:16).

In Jerusalem and Judea the Jewish mission was remarkably successful, but in the wider Greco-Roman world the number of converts from the synagogue was insignificant by comparison with the number of converts from paganism. Less than twenty years after the death and resurrection of Christ the number of Gentiles in the church as a whole was rapidly exceeding the number of Jews: it was this situation, indeed, which made the Council of Jerusalem necessary. By the end of a further period of twenty years, the church throughout the world was a predominantly Gentile society, thanks largely to Paul's energetic prosecution of his apostolic task.

Paul had not been called to evangelize Jews, but indirectly he believed that his ministry to Gentiles would promote the salvation of Israel. Indeed, he says plainly that a primary reason for his magnifying his office as apostle to the Gentiles was his hope that the Gentiles' enjoyment of the blessings of the gospel would provoke his fellow-Israelites to envy and impel them to claim their natural share in these blessings. So far as the *presentation* of the gospel was concerned, the order was "to the Jew first and also to the Greek," but so far as its *acceptance* was concerned, the order was reversed: "by the Gentile first, and then by the Jew." From Paul's perspective, the large-scale turning of Israel to Christ would apparently be the consummating stage in the divine program for human history. When the sum-total of Gentile believers had come into the fellowship of the people of God, this would be the means by which all Israel would enter into salvation, its temporary blindness removed. Paul's own ministry, then, both in its direct effect upon Gentiles and in its indirect implications for Jews, was an instrument in God's hands for the accomplishment of His saving purpose in Christ. The advent of Christ could not come until Paul's task was finished.

That the Gentiles should have priority over the Jews in the receiving of the promised blessings of the messianic age, even if only in point of time, was an idea so unprecedented and indeed so preposterous that it required the firmest possible validation. For Paul, the experience of his ministry might have been validation enough, but he invokes stronger validation when he imparts as a "mystery" to the Christians in Rome the teaching that "a hardening has come upon part of Israel, until the full number of the Gentiles come in, and so all Israel will be saved" (Rom.

11:25f.). The renovated people of God will embrace both Jews and Gentiles, although for the present its constitution is predominantly Gentile. The prophets of Israel had adumbrated this course of salvation-history, but a further revelation—the "mystery" of Romans 11:25—was necessary to show clearly how their predictions were to be fulfilled.

But here and now, even if Jews were a minority in the new community, this minority formed part of the community, and indeed comprised its foundation members. What was the relation of believing Jews in the church to the Gentile majority?

The answer to this question is given in the unfolding of a further, or fuller, "mystery"—the "mystery" of the union of Jewish and Gentile believers as fellow members of the body of Christ.

In his earlier letters—more particularly in I Corinthians 12:12-27 and Romans 12:4-8—Paul uses the figure of the body of Christ as a simile or metaphor to illustrate the corporate life of Christians. As the various parts of the body discharge their proper functions for the well-being of the whole, so individual Christians fulfill their respective ministries for the well-being of the community. The Roman Christians are called "one body in Christ" (Rom. 12:5); the Corinthian Christians similarly are "the body of Christ and individually members of it" (I Cor. 12:27). Into this one body they had been baptized in one Spirit, all of them, "Jews or Greeks, slaves or free" (I Cor. 12:13). Similarly the Galatian Christians are told that for those who have been "baptized into Christ" there is "neither Jew nor Greek, neither slave nor free, neither male nor female" but all are "one in Christ Jesus" (Gal. 3:27f.). Whatever differences had existed between them before they became Christians were irrelevant in the new community; but of those differences the one which Paul took most seriously was that between Jews and Gentiles, for this difference had a religious basis. He himself, to whom the privileges of the chosen people had formerly been matters for pride, to be defended with jealous care, had now become the foremost champion of equal rights for Gentiles within the fellowship of the people of God, and by his ministry did more than any of his contemporaries to break down in practice the "middle wall of partition" which had separated Jews from Gentiles, as Christ by His death on the cross had broken it down in principle (Eph. 2:14).

In Colossians and Ephesians this new unity which Jews and Gentiles have in Christ is emphasized by means of the "body" terminology. The church, not only locally but in its universal aspect, is now the body of Christ in the sense that it is the body of which the risen Christ is the head; the life which animates the body is the risen life of Christ, imparted from Him through the Spirit to the worldwide community and to all its members. Years before these later letters were written, Paul could say that "it is no longer I who live, but Christ who lives in me; and the life I now live in the flesh I live by faith in the Son of God" (Gal. 2:20). But now the relation between the body and the head supplies the most effective terminology which Paul can find to express this vital faith-union with Christ.

It has been suggested already that the seed of this idea was sown in Paul's mind on the Damascus road, when the voice from heaven, saying "why are you persecuting me?" (Acts 9:4, etc.), indicated that the risen Lord accepted as done to Himself whatever was done to His people on earth. The idea in any case would come the more naturally to Paul because of the ready oscillation in Hebrew thought between individual and corporate personality. But it also provided a framework within which the new unity between Jewish and Gentile believers could find adequate expression, and in this connection the word "mystery" appears again, with special relation to Paul's distinctive ministry.

In Colossians 1:26f. Paul describes the message which he has been commissioned to deliver as "the mystery hidden for ages and generations but now made manifest to his saints." "To them," he adds, "God chose to make known how great among the Gentiles are the riches of the glory of this mystery, which is Christ in you, the hope of glory."

The saving purpose of the God of Israel was a major theme of Old Testament prophets, some of whom had also foretold how Gentiles as well as Israelites would come within its scope. But the manner in which this would be realized—by the incorporation of Gentile and Jewish believers on an equal footing in the community which shared the life of the risen Christ— was not made known. This had remained concealed within the divine counsels until the time of its accomplishment. Now Paul, to whom this "mystery" has been disclosed, unfolds its wonder to his readers that they may be moved to worship God for the glory of His rich grace thus lavishly dispensed. Had this grace been displayed to Jewish believers only, it would still have been grace, but it might not have excited such wonder: the Jews were already known to be the objects of God's gracious choice. But Gentile believers also are included, and on the same terms as

Jewish believers; and it is Paul's great joy, as it is his divinely imposed commission, to be the steward of this "mystery" as the Gentiles' apostle. "Christ is in you," he assures his friends at Colossae; "Christ is in you [even in you Gentiles] as your hope of glory." The fact that here and now, as fully incorporated members of the body of Christ, they had a share in His resurrection life, afforded them the sure hope that, on the day of the "revealing of the sons of God" (Rom. 8:19), they would share in His manifested glory. Christ is Himself the center and circumference of this "mystery"; by His death and exaltation He has unleashed the process which brings this eternal purpose of God to ultimate realization, and those who are united to Christ are involved in its realization—in measure now, in fullness at His advent in glory.

Paul's stewardship of this mystery is further described in Ephesians 3:1-12, where he expresses his sense of wonder that to him of all people (in view of his past record) the privilege should have been granted of proclaiming to the Gentiles "the unsearchable riches of Christ" and thereby bringing to light the long-concealed plan of God—bringing it to light not only in the eyes of men but in the sight of "the principalities and powers in the heavenly places," for whom the church serves as an object lesson of "the manifold wisdom of God." For the church of the new creation presents an aspect of the divine wisdom unparalleled in the old creation: in it Gentile believers are fellow heirs with Jewish believers of all the covenanted mercies of God.

The Mystery of God's Final Purpose

No cleavage within the human family was so basic in Paul's ancestral thinking as that between Jew and Gentile. If this cleavage could be obliterated in Christ, so could any and every other cleavage. There are other cleavages within the human family today which may appear more unbridgeable than that between Jew and Gentile. But the lesson of the Letter to the Ephesians is that all of them can be, and will be, overcome in Christ. The church itself is not the final phase of God's plan for mankind: it is God's pilot scheme for the final phase, for "the mystery of his will," a purpose which has its origin and its consummation in Christ, is set forth as "a plan for the fulness of time, to unite all things in him, things in heaven and things on earth" (Eph. 1:9f.). The church, God's masterpiece of reconciliation, is to provide the pattern for the reconciled universe of the future, when all things will find their unity under Christ as their true head; the church is also called to be God's instrument in promoting this consummation. Of course, if the cleavages which occur outside the church are reproduced inside the church, then the church fails to play its part in the furtherance of the divine purpose. But since this purpose was conceived "in Christ," its realization "in Christ" is assured. Nothing less than this is the "mystery of God's will, now unfolded in the gospel.

All this is involved in the gospel which came to Paul on the Damascus road "through a revelation of Jesus Christ" (Gal. 1:12). How long it was before its details became clear in Paul's mind we cannot be sure, but he did not receive this "insight into the mystery of Christ" from those who were in Christ before him. It is bound up with the understanding and fulfillment of his call to proclaim among the Gentiles the Son of God who was revealed to him on the Damascus road—that is to say, with his knowledge of Jesus as the exalted Lord. Yet the exalted Lord, with whom Paul enjoyed immediate acquaintance, was in his mind identical and continuous with the historical Jesus, with whom he had not enjoyed such acquaintance.

3

Paul's Gospel as Tradition

In counterpoise to the gospel as revelation in Paul's writings, stands the gospel as tradition. Whereas the gospel as revelation relates to the personal revelation of Christ to the apostle or to his discernment and disclosure of God's hidden purpose, the gospel as tradition relates to historical facts, depending on the testimony of eyewitnesses. Or, we might say, the gospel as revelation relates to the present ministry of the exalted Lord who shares His risen life with His people on earth, while the gospel as tradition relates to the earthly ministry of Jesus—provided we remember that it is one and the same Jesus who is active in the successive phases of His ministry.

The gospel as tradition emerges with special clarity where the technical terminology of tradition is used by Paul—either the noun "tradition" (*paradosis*) itself or the correlative verbs "receive" (*paralambanō*) and "deliver" (*paradidōmi*)—in reference to a chain of information or instruction handed down from one to another. The idea of tradition was familiar to Paul in his earlier days; the question now was: which is the valid tradition —the tradition of the elders, which he had formerly received, or the tradition of Christ?

When Paul tells the Galatians how "extremely zealous" he was in his earlier years for "the traditions of my fathers" (Gal. 1:14), he would include in these traditions the interpretation of

41

the law handed down in the school of Hillel of which, after
the founder's death, Gamaliel was principal. But with his conversion to Christianity, these traditions were replaced in his life
by something which he recognized to be better. Paul was not the
only Pharisee to become a Christian, but his conversion involved a much more radical reorientation than was experienced
by those of his fellow-Pharisees whose reaction to the news of
the evangelization of Gentiles was that it was "necessary to
circumcise them, and to charge them to keep the law of Moses"
(Acts 15:5). For Paul, "the law of Moses from Sinai" gave way
to what, in his own words, he "received from the Lord" (I Cor.
11:23)—to a new tradition stemming not from Moses but from
Christ.

When Paul speaks of this Christian tradition, it apparently
comprises three main elements which, in ascending order of
importance, may be listed thus: ethical and procedural rules;
words and deeds of Christ; the basic Christian message, in which
special emphasis was laid on the death and resurrection of Christ.

Ethical and Procedural Rules

"Stand firm," Paul writes to the Thessalonians, "and hold to
the traditions which you were taught by us, either by word of
mouth or by letter" (II Thess. 2:15). These traditions were
thoroughly practical in character, if we may judge from II Thessalonians 3:6, where Paul solemnly enjoins his readers to "keep
away from any brother who is living in idleness and not in
accord with the tradition that you received from us." The "tradition that you received from us" in this connection was imparted
by examples as well as by precept; it is summed up in the ruling:
"If any one will not work, let him not eat" (II Thess. 3:10).

Again Paul commends the Corinthian Christians because, as
he says, "you remember me in everything and maintain the
traditions even as I have delivered them to you" (I Cor. 11:2).
This is probably his response to an assurance conveyed to him
in their letter: "We remember you in everything and maintain
the traditions even as you have delivered them to us." "That's
fine," says Paul; but to his commendation he adds some words
suggesting that he is not completely satisfied with their assurance.
For example, in the matter of the veiling or non-veiling of their
heads at church meetings, they were out of step both with the
instruction which Paul had given them and with the practice of
other churches. More serious than that was their departure

from the elementary dictates of Christian charity by their selfish conduct at the communion meal, which made a mockery of their claim to eat the Lord's supper. "Shall I commend you in this? I will not" (I Cor. 11:22).

These practical instructions are called "traditions," but they may be traditions only in the sense that Paul delivered them to his churches, not in the sense that he had received them from others. Tradition must begin somewhere, and occasionally it might begin with Paul's own example and teaching. In such cases it provides no obvious link between Paul and the historical Jesus. But his rebuke of the Corinthians for their unbrotherly behavior at the communion meal leads him to remind them of a tradition which does stem from Jesus.

Words and Deeds of Christ

An excellent example of this second form of tradition, which provides a firm link with the historical Jesus, is the narrative in I Corinthians 11:23-25 of the institution of the Lord's Supper "on the night when he was betrayed." Paul does not here relate this narrative to the Corinthian Christians for the first time; he reminds them of something he had "delivered" to them when he founded their church five years previously—something which he himself had already "received from the Lord." This phraseology need not imply *direct* communication; but it does mean that the Lord is the source of this tradition, not only in the sense that He is the originator of the chain of tradition but also in the sense that, from His present state of glory, He maintains and validates the tradition by His Spirit.[1]

The narrative which Paul here reproduces plainly goes back to the same source as the narrative of Mark 14:22-24 and its parallels in Matthew and Luke. Paul's version, even in its written form, is ten years earlier than Mark's; even so, Mark's version may preserve some more archaic features. Thus, the words of Jesus in Mark 14:25 ("I shall not drink again of the fruit of the vine until that day when I drink it new in the kingdom of God") may be paraphrased or summarized in Paul's own words "until he comes," in I Corinthians 11:26. Again, some features of Paul's narrative (such as the injunction "Do this . . . in remembrance of me") are akin to the longer text of Luke 22:17-20, which seems to combine an independent, shorter version with another version related to that which Paul quotes.

---

1. Cf. O. Cullmann, *The Early Church* (London, 1956), pp. 66ff.

A comparative study of the respective versions leads to some interesting conclusions about eucharistic origins, but this is not our present concern. The version reproduced by Paul is probably that which was used in the communities where he first enjoyed Christian fellowship. Since it related what "the Lord Jesus" did and said, including the injunction which He laid upon His followers, it was a tradition "received from the Lord" and accordingly delivered by Paul to his converts. The core of the narrative (as distinct from interpretative additions) was probably preserved with little change because it was constantly repeated in church meetings as often as Christians "ate this bread and drank the cup," together with the repetition of the passion story itself —"you proclaim the Lord's death," says Paul (I Cor. 11:26).

The Basic Christian Message

The passion story itself soon acquired firm outlines from its being constantly repeated not only at celebrations of the Lord's Supper but also as part of the proclamation of the gospel. For the basic Christian message laid special emphasis on the death and resurrection of Christ. According to Paul, "Jesus Christ was publicly portrayed as crucified" when the gospel was preached (Gal. 3:1), and equally on every such occasion Christ was "preached as raised from the dead" (I Cor. 15:12).

That the preaching of Christ crucified and risen belonged to the tradition shared by Paul with the other apostles is evident from I Corinthians 15:3-11 where, in turning to deal with those members of the Corinthian church who denied the resurrection of the dead, Paul reminds that church of the gospel which brought them salvation when first he visited the city. "I delivered to you as of first importance what I also received," he says, "that Christ died for our sins in accordance with the scriptures, that he was buried, that he was raised on the third day in accordance with the scriptures, and that he appeared to Cephas, then to the twelve. . . ."

Paul wrote this to the Corinthians about A.D. 55, not more than twenty-five years after the events in question, but evidently he had communicated the content of this "tradition" to them by word of mouth five years earlier. If we remove his personal contribution from what he delivered to them (such as verse 8, "Last of all, . . . he appeared to me also"), what is left is what Paul himself had "received" several years before that.

He knew, of course, about Jesus' death before his conversion, while the risen Lord revealed Himself to him immediately on the

Damascus road. But the outline of the primitive message, as he transmits it here, was something which he shared with his predecessors, while some of the historical details of the message were for the first time imparted to him by one or another of those predecessors. It has been suggested that he learned the outline in one of the churches with which he had fellowship in his earlier Christian days, such as Damascus or Antioch. We need not stay to discuss this here, as we shall see that Paul's own formulation of the outline indicates clearly enough who his principal informants were.

The outline falls into four parts, each introduced by the conjunction "that":

>   (i) that Christ died . . . ,
>   (ii) that He was buried . . . ,
>   (iii) that He was raised . . . ,
>   (iv) that He appeared . . .

The fourth of these clauses is expanded more than the others, even in Paul's compressed outline (this is no doubt related to the purpose for which the outline is introduced), but in actual preaching each of them would be amplified with substantial detail. It may be that the first and third clauses could be considered as primary in importance ("Christ died . . . and . . . was raised . . ."), while the second and fourth are appended respectively to the first and third ("Christ died . . . and . . . was buried"; "he was raised . . . and . . . appeared . . ."); but in view of Paul's expansion of the fourth clause this should not be pressed.

(i) The first clause states "that Christ died for our sins in accordance with the scriptures." Does the whole of this clause belong to the tradition, or does part of it represent Paul's interpretation of the tradition? Certainly the phrase "in accordance with the scriptures" reflects a primitive emphasis in the gospel story: in the earliest form of it which we can trace, the element of fulfillment of prophecy is stressed. Mark introduces "the beginning of the gospel" with prophetic quotations, and tells how Jesus submitted to His captors with the words: "Let the scriptures be fulfilled" (14:49). If "the scriptures" in accordance with which "Christ died" could be held to include the fourth Isaianic servant song, then we recall that the Servant's life is given as a guilt offering and that He bears "the sin of many" (Isa. 53:10-12)—in which case the phrase "for our sins" might also belong to the tradition. Although the atoning aspect of the death of Christ is not prominent in Acts, it has a central place in Paul's teaching, and may well have belonged to the tradition which Paul "received."

The question of a Semitic substratum to this clause, which has been debated by Joachim Jeremias and others, is not of the first importance.[2] If we are told that the Greek phrase "in accordance with the scriptures" has no Aramaic equivalent, we may rightly doubt whether it was in fact impossible to express such an idea in Aramaic; and in any case it does not matter. Paul delivered the outline to his converts in Greek, and even if he "received" it in Aramaic, he was not bound to reproduce it in a literal translation.

One phase of the debate about the Semitic substratum concentrates on the fact that *Christ* is used here without the Greek article.[3] More important is the fact that the word *Christ* is used at all. Its use here reminds us that the most primitive form of the apostolic message insisted that Jesus was the Messiah. If a pagan said "Christ died" (as Tacitus, for example, practically does),[4] he would simply be making a statement of fact: to him "Christ" would be nothing more than an alternative name for Jesus. But for Jews like Paul and has predecessors to say "Christ died" involves more than a statement of fact; it includes an assessment of the person who died, an affirmation that He was the Lord's anointed (*christos* being, like Hebrew *mashiach*, a verbal adjective meaning "anointed"). Three theological propositions are therefore contained in this clause: (1) the person who died was the Messiah; (2) He endured death for His people's sins; (3) His death took place in accordance with Old Testament Scripture.

(ii) The second clause states that Christ "was buried." It may surprise us that His burial is given a clause to itself, but this suggests that it was an independent feature in the tradition. What then is the significance of its separate mention? There is, of course, the point that burial is sometimes added to death to confirm its reality and underline its finality. "David both died and was buried," says Peter on the day of Pentecost, "and his tomb is with us to this day" (Acts 2:29). But more than this is implied here, with the repetition of the conjunction "that" be-

---

2. Cf. *The Eucharistic Words of Jesus* (Oxford, 1955), pp. 129ff.

3. Cf. J. Jeremias, "Artikelloses *Christos*," *Zeitschrift für die neutestamentliche Wissenschaft* 57 (1966), pp. 211ff.; "Nochmals: Artikelloses *Christos*," ibid. 60 (1969), pp. 215ff.

4. *Annals* xv. 44.

fore "He was buried." It is implied that the raising, which is
mentioned next, was the reversal of the burying, and this points
to the motif of the empty tomb. "What he [Paul] has to say
about the resurrection of Jesus in I Cor. 15 clearly implies that
he did not believe that the body of the Lord remained in the
grave. The absence, however, of any reference to the fact that
the grave was empty, shows that he did not regard it as a proof
of the resurrection."⁵ One could not infer that Jesus had come
back to life from the fact that His body was missing from the
tomb; but if His body had still been there, that would have been
proof enough that He had not been raised from the dead in the
sense which this language bore in Jewish circles in the first
century A.D.

(iii) The third clause states that Christ "was raised on the
third day in accordance with the scriptures." How much of this
belonged to the tradition which Paul originally received—all of
it, or only part?

The note of fulfillment of prophecy seems to have been as
constant in the apostolic preaching of the resurrection as it was
in the apostolic preaching of the cross, and when the time of the
resurrection is mentioned in the apostolic preaching, it is regularly given as the third day. But nowhere in our accounts of the
apostolic preaching have we a statement that the prophetic
Scriptures point to the third day as the day of resurrection.
Have we such a statement here?

Perhaps we have, but if so it is not easy to say with certainty
which prophetic Scriptures are in view. The one most commonly cited in Hosea 6:2, "After two days he will revive us; on
the third day he will raise us up, that we may live before him";
but the relevance of this to Jesus' resurrection is not immediately
obvious. Even less obvious is the relevance of II Kings 20:5,
where Hezekiah is told: "on the third day you shall go up to the
house of the Lord." Sometimes other Old Testament texts have
been cited in which "the third day" is not explicitly mentioned.
Jonah's being "in the belly of the fish three days and three
nights" (Jonah 1:17) can scarcely come into the picture here,
as it does in Matthew 12:40, because of the *prima facie* difference between that extent of time and what is implied in "the
third day." An attractive suggestion, in view of what is said
about Christ as "the first fruits of those who have fallen asleep"
in I Corinthians 15:20, is that Paul has in mind Leviticus 23:9-

---

5. S. H. Hooke, *The Resurrection of Christ* (London, 1967), p. 114.

21, where the "sheaf of the first fruits" is "waved before the Lord on "the morrow after the sabbath" following Passover. But "the morrow after the sabbath" (i.e., Sunday) would be the third day only where the Passover was sacrificed on a Friday (as in fact it was in the year of our Lord's crucifixion), and it is doubtful if Paul would have adduced a Scripture which does not necessarily point to the third day.

In an article published in the *Journal of Theological Studies* in 1957,[6] B. M. Metzger argued that this third clause in Paul's outline actually comprises two separate statements:

(1) He was raised from the dead in accordance with the Scriptures.

(2) He was raised from the dead on the third day.

If these two statements are separate, then there need be no direct relation between "in accordance with scriptures" and "on the third day." We are in that case not restricted to Scriptures which speak expressly or by implication of the third day, and we might therefore think, for example, of such a text as Psalm 16:10 ("Thou wilt not abandon my soul to Hades . . ."), quoted in this connection in Acts 2:27 and 13:35.

As for the phrase "on the third day," this is regularly used after the resurrection when the time of its occurrence is indicated. In pre-resurrection contexts, "after three days" occurs (not to mention the "three days and three nights" of Matt. 12:40). The phrase "after three days," used for example, in Mark 8:31 ("the Son of Man must suffer many things . . . and be killed, and after three days rise again"), may be a general expression meaning "in a short time." The constancy of "on the third day" in contexts after the event reflects the fact that it was actually on the third day that Christ rose from the dead.

(iv) The fourth clause begins with the statement that Christ "appeared to Cephas, then to the twelve."

On the location of the resurrection appearances which he lists, Paul has nothing to say. We may try to decide where some of them took place by identifying them with appearances recorded in the Gospels, but this is a precarious proceeding except in the case of one or two. Perhaps Paul's list includes both Judean and Galilean appearances, but we cannot be sure.

What purpose did this list of appearances serve — not so much in its present context in the letter as in the apostolic tradition

6. "A Suggestion Concerning the Meaning of I Cor. xv. 4b," *Journal of Theological Studies*, new series 8 (1957), pp. 118ff.

proclaimed at Corinth and elsewhere? The natural answer is that the appearances were adduced to confirm the reality of the resurrection. "The early Christians," it has been rightly said, "did not believe in the resurrection of Christ because they could not find his dead body. They believed because they did find a living Christ."[7] And they endeavored to communicate their assurance that Christ was risen by telling others what they had seen and heard.

This account of the matter, however, is not universally admitted. Karl Barth maintained that "verses 5-7 have nothing to do with supplying a historical proof." Paul contended rather "for his apostolic method, of which he cannot concede that it was perhaps only *his* method, and for this reason he now conjures up the cloud of witnesses, *not* to confirm the fact of the resurrection of Jesus . . . but to confirm that the foundation of the Church, so far as the eye can see, can be traced back to nothing else than appearances of the risen Christ."[8]

Rudolf Bultmann saw, however, that Barth's attempt "to explain away the real meaning of I Cor. 15" could not hold water. He himself agrees that in this one place Paul—uncharacteristically!—"tries to prove the miracle of the resurrection by adducing a list of eye-witnesses." But this he regards as "a dangerous procedure";[9] after all, "an historical fact which involves a resurrection from the dead is utterly inconceivable!"[10] (It is inconceivable, of course, only to those whose presuppositions exclude any such thing.)

Paul adduces the list of eyewitnesses as testimony to the resurrection fact, and draws a clear distinction between the resurrection fact and the resurrection faith. The fact is antecedent to the faith; the faith depends on the fact. Without the fact, the faith is futile: "if Christ has not been raised, then . . . your faith is in vain" (I Cor. 15:14).

The testimony of eyewitnesses was highly regarded in antiquity. It was reckoned of great value in Roman law, as it is in many areas of modern law and also among unsophisticated people who appreciate the immediacy of an "I was there" account. No wonder, then, that it played a prominent part in the primitive apostolic preaching; the summaries of speeches in Acts provide repeated evidence of this.

---

7. C. T. Craig, *The Beginning of Christianity* (New York, 1943), p. 135.
8. *The Resurrection of the Dead* (1933), p. 150.
9. The adjective in Bultmann's original German is *fatal*.
10. *Kerygma and Myth,* ed. H. W. Bartsch (London, 1953), p. 39.

According to important strands in the Gospel narratives, it was to women, and more particularly to Mary Magdalene, that the risen Christ first made Himself known. But no reference was made to these appearances in the apostolic preaching. Although much store was set by eyewitness testimony in general, the testimony of women was reckoned as of little or no account, and to adduce it publicly would have weakened, not strengthened, the case for the resurrection. This is illustrated by a remark of the second-century anti-Christian writer Celsus, who traced the resurrection witness back to "the ravings of a hysterical woman" (meaning Mary Magdalene) and dismissed it accordingly as unworthy of serious attention.[11]

What is emphasized in the apostolic preaching is the appearances of the risen Christ to the responsible leaders of the Christian movement. Two of these leaders—Cephas (Peter) and James—are mentioned by name in Paul's list. The mention of these two leaders calls to mind the twofold view expressed by Adolf Harnack[12] and developed by B. W. Bacon:[13] (1) that Cephas and James stand at the head of two short lists—(a) Cephas, the twelve, more than 500 brethren at one time; (b) James, all the apostles; and (2) that these two lists represent two parallel, if not rival, traditions—(a) a Petrine and Galilean tradition; (b) a Jacobean and Jerusalem tradition.

But one can scarcely avoid linking the reference to Cephas and James here with Paul's other reference to the two of them in Galatians 1:18f. where he says that three years after his conversion "I went up to Jerusalem to visit Cephas, and remained with him fifteen days; but I saw none of the other apostles except James the Lord's brother." This points to the occasion when Paul "received" this tradition: it was not in Damascus or Antioch or any of the Hellenistic communities; it was in Jerusalem, during his first visit there after his conversion. Cephas and James both told him how each of them had seen the risen Lord, while he in turn told them how he also had seen Him, belatedly but none the less really.

But if Paul acquired this information so early as *ca.* A.D. 35, there was hardly time by then for two parallel or rival traditions to crystallize. The first part of the Harnack-Bacon hypo-

---

11. Quoted by Origen, *Against Celsus* ii. 59.

12. *Sitzungsbericht der preussischen Akademie der Wissenschaften,* phil.-hist. Klasse (Berlin, 1922), pp. 62ff.

13. *The Apostolic Message* (New York, 1925), pp. 132ff.; *The Story of Jesus* (London, 1928), pp. 304ff.

thesis, however, is quite credible: the two names respectively introduce two short lists. In the former "the twelve" are mentioned after their leader, Peter, just as "all the apostles" (a wider circle than the twelve in Paul's terminology) are mentioned after James who, according to the most probable interpretation of Galatians 1:19, was himself an apostle, though not one of the twelve. The repetition of "then" in I Corinthians 15:5-7 suggests that the appearance of the risen Lord to James followed His appearance to Cephas.

That on this occasion Paul went up to Jerusalem—in part, at least— to acquire such information is suggested by the verb "to visit" (as RSV translates it); for *historēsai Kēphan* implies "to make inquiry of Peter." It is most probable, then, that it was at this time that Paul "received" the details of the tradition which he delivered to his Corinthian converts twenty years later.

The appearance of the risen Lord to Peter is attested independently in Luke 24:34, where the two disciples from Emmaus, returning late on Easter Day to the eleven and their companions at their headquarters in Jerusalem, are greeted by them with the news: "The Lord has been raised indeed, and has appeared to Simon"—an archaic fragment, unaccompanied by any attempt to describe His appearance to Simon. The adverb "indeed" (*ontōs*) implies a previous doubt, associated with the women's report. The disciples could not bring themselves to accept the women's testimony (Luke 24:11, 22) but, if the Lord had appeared to *Simon,* that was different: He had been raised indeed.

Nothing was so calculated to confirm Peter's primacy among the apostles (*inter pares,* of course) as the fact that he was the first of them to see the Lord in resurrection. Even if the "you are Peter" pericope of Matthew 16:17-19 belongs historically to its literary setting in the region of Caesarea Philippi and not to this resurrection appearance, an earlier bestowal of primacy might nevertheless have been held to be cancelled by Peter's denial in the courtyard of the high priest's palace. A post-resurrection confirmation, or re-confirmation, was what was required to set all doubts on this score at rest.

The appearance to "the twelve," which follows that to Peter, is perhaps identical with the appearance of Luke 24:36 (cf. John 20:19), since Jesus (according to Luke) had already "appeared to Simon" before He "stood among" the eleven and their companions in Jerusalem. "The eleven" and "the twelve" are, of course, the same group; any one who wished to contest the point might be reminded that Matthias (cf. Acts 1:21-26) was probably one of "those who were with" the eleven on the occasion in question. Moreover, "the twelve" are mentioned naturally after Peter, their leader. But if this identification is well founded, we can scarcely adopt the view that we have a "Galilean" tradition here, unless Luke (with John) has replaced what was originally a Galilean setting by a Jerusalem one—for which there is no evidence.

As for the appearance to "more than five hundred brethren at one time," it cannot easily be equated with any occasion recorded in the Gospels or Acts. It has been identified (e.g., tentatively, by T. C. Edwards)[14] with the Galilean appearance announced in Matthew 28:10 and (e.g., by E. von Dobschütz and F. C. Burkitt)[15] with the Pentecostal experience of Acts 2. But the appearance announced in Matthew 28:10 is certainly to be identified with that described in Matthew 28:16-20, and there is no suggestion in Matthew 28:16 that "the eleven disciples" were accompanied by any other followers of Jesus, while the attempted identification with the experience of Acts 2 (where there is no word of an appearance of the risen Christ) would imply that one at least of the two accounts has deviated from the original form to a point where all basis for a comparison or identification disappears. It is best to conclude that this element in the tradition is recorded in I Corinthians 15:6 only and nowhere else in the New Testament. That it should be unmentioned in the Gospels is not such "an incredible supposition" as Sir Robert Anderson thought.[16]

The appearance to James is equally unmentioned in the Gospels. Yet such an appearance helps to explain how James and the other brothers of the Lord, though not included among His disciples before His death, and perhaps quite positively opposed to Him (cf. John 7:5; Mark 3:21, 31-35), appear both in Luke and in Paul as prominent figures among the Christian leaders from the earliest post-resurrection period onwards (cf. Acts 1:14; I Cor. 9:5). In some Jewish-Christian circles the

---

14. *A Commentary on the First Epistle to the Corinthians* (London, 1897), p. 396; the appearance, he adds, "must have been after the day of Pentecost, when the disciples numbered a hundred and twenty."

15. E. von Dobschütz, *Ostern und Pfingsten* (Leipzig, 1903); F. C. Burkitt, *Christian Beginnings* (London, 1924), pp. 90ff. Several other writers have followed their lead.

16. *The Buddha of Christendom* (London, 1899), p. 271. He identifies the occasion with the appearance of Matthew 28:16-20.

appearance of the risen Lord to James played a specially significant part, as is indicated by the fragment quoted by Jerome
from the Gospel according to the Hebrews:

> When the Lord had given the linen cloth to the servant of
> the priest, He went to James and appeared to him. For James
> had sworn that from that hour in which he had drunk the cup
> of the Lord he would eat no bread until he should see Him
> risen from among those who sleep. And shortly after that the
> Lord said: "Bring a table and bread!" Immediately it is
> added: "He took the bread, blessed it and broke it and gave
> it to James the Just, saying, 'My brother, eat your bread, for
> the Son of Man is risen from among those who sleep.' "[17]

The legendary embellishments are easily recognized, such as
the implication that James had been present at the Last Supper.
But the core of the passage is confirmed by the tradition which
Paul received probably in the third year from his conversion:
the risen Lord "appeared to James." (The motif of the risen
Lord's providing or blessing food for His followers is found in
Luke 24:30 and John 21:9ff.)

Is there any special significance in the word "all" when Paul,
after speaking of the risen Lord's appearance to James, adds
that He appeared next after that to "all the apostles"? R. H.
Fuller has found such a significance in the light of the fact that
there were two groups among the apostles, one Aramaic-speaking
and the other Hellenistic: the phrase "all the apostles," he suggests, includes both groups. The appearances to Peter and the
twelve, he holds, had a church-founding significance; those to
James and "all the apostles" had a mission-founding significance
—both the Aramaic-speaking mission in Palestine and the Hellenistic mission in Phoenicia, Cyprus, and Antioch being in
view.[18] A simpler explanation would be that Paul, who uses the
term "apostles" to include more than the twelve—to include, for
example, himself (I Cor. 15:9) and James (Gal. 1:19), not to
mention people like Andronicus and Junias (Rom. 16:7)—
mentions *"all* the apostles" by way of emphasizing that more
than the twelve were involved.

This concludes the tradition which Paul received from others.
His own contribution to the tradition originated in his personal
experience. But while it began with him—or rather, as he would
have said, with the risen Lord who appeared to him—it was

17. Jerome, *On Illustrious Men*, 2.
18. *The Formation of the Resurrection Narratives* (London, 1972),
p. 41.

henceforth fed into the ongoing stream of tradition, as Paul delivered it to his converts, and added to the earlier appearances as the one which concluded the series.

It is implied that the appearance to Paul was of the same order as the appearances to those who were in Christ before him. The same occasion is described elsewhere in a variety of terms. "Have I not seen Jesus our Lord?" he asks in I Corinthians 9:1. God "was pleased to reveal his Son to me," he says in Galatians 1:16, and the reference to Damascus later in the same sentence (1:17) confirms that this is the Damascus road experience described in Acts 9:1ff. "I was apprehended by Christ Jesus" is how he puts it in Philippians 3:12. Here, however, in I Corinthians 15:8 he uses the passive *ōphthē* (as he uses it of the appearances to his predecessors) in what grammarians might call a tolerative sense. Christ is not only the grammatical subject (as is inevitable when the verb is passive); He is the real subject or agent: "He let Himself be seen." Had He not taken the initiative, none of those mentioned would have seen Him. In using the same construction of himself as of the others, Paul indicates not that their experience was as "visionary" as his, but that his was as "real" as theirs.

It is further implied that the resurrection body in which Christ appeared to them all is of the same order as the resurrection body to which the people of Christ look forward—that is to say, a "spiritual body" (I Cor. 15:44) or a "body of glory" (Phil. 3:21). It was, then, in such a body that Christ, having now become in resurrection the "man of heaven" and a "life-giving spirit" (I Cor. 15:45-49), showed Himself to His disciples, albeit in a form which was accommodated to their earthly vision. The body of flesh and blood, which was laid in the tomb, was evidently transmuted without remainder into His body of glory, in which He appeared to Peter, James and the others, and last of all to Paul himself.

Paul's gospel as tradition, then, bridges whatever gulf may separate the historical Jesus from the risen Lord, for it includes both within its scope, and affirms the continuity and identity of the one with the other.

4

The Way of Salvation

We have to acknowledge that in Paul's letters there is a remarkable absence of reference to details of Christ's ministry. Whereas in the First Letter of Peter, Jesus' patient and uncomplaining behavior in the face of injustice and ill-treatment is presented as an example for Christians to follow (even though the language is considerably influenced by Isaiah 53), Paul is more prone in similar circumstances to present the example of Christ's condescension and self-humiliation in becoming man: for him the *imitatio Christi* is mainly a matter, in B. B. Warfield's phrase, of "imitating the Incarnation."[1]

It may be said, and with some truth, that Paul's readers had already heard and believed the story of Jesus, and did not need to be told it again. In Acts 13:23ff., in the report of his preaching in the synagogue at Pisidian Antioch, Paul is represented as following up his account of Old Testament history and prophecy with a reference to the ministry of John the Baptist, represented elsewhere in the New Testament as the initial phase of the kerygma; and this may well be in keeping with Paul's practice. But the principal reason for the lack of allusion to the events of Jesus' ministry may quite simply be that Paul was not an

---

1. *The Person and Work of Christ* (Philadelphia, 1950), pp. 563ff.

eyewitness of these events, and preferred to confine himself to those matters of which he could speak at first hand.

"In the future," wrote Victor P. Furnish in an article published in 1965, "scholars must concentrate not on what or how much Paul knew about the historical Jesus, but rather on the way he employed and applied the knowledge he did have, and what place the Jesus of history had in relation to the heart and centre of his preaching."[2]

Paul's relation to Jesus (in addition to his personal incorporation, with all his fellow-believers, "in Christ") may be established more securely at a deeper level than that represented by such allusions as can be picked up throughout his letters to the life and teaching of Jesus. If Paul's claim to "have the mind of Christ" (I Cor. 2:16) is well founded, then we may confidently turn to the letters of Paul to find the significance of the Jesus of history unfolded. To that significance Jesus Himself pointed when He spoke of the divine kingdom which was both present and imminent; what was imminent when He spoke had become an accomplished fact by the time Paul wrote, and in expounding the implications of this accomplished fact Paul unfolds the significance of Jesus. Some people who talk as if the significance of the *historical* Jesus is unrelated to anything that happened after His death overlook the fact that the significance of any outstanding figure of history would not adequately be brought out if the sequel to his life and death were strictly excluded from the reckoning. From Jesus' own teaching we should gather that the inauguration of the kingdom and the vindication of the Son of Man would illuminate features of His works and words which at the time presented a mystery; Paul, writing from the perspective of that inauguration and vindication, makes the mystery plain.

Justification by Grace

Nowhere has Paul more fully entered into the heart of Jesus' teaching about God and man than in his insistence on justification by divine grace. "Nowhere," says Joachim Jeremias, "is the connection between Paul and Jesus so evident as here."[3] For this is a principle which recurs repeatedly in Jesus' parables. (A far

---

2. "The Jesus-Paul Debate: From Baur to Bultmann," *Bulletin of the John Rylands Library* 47 (1964-65), p. 381.
3. "Paul and James," *Expository Times* 66 (1954-55), p. 369.

cry indeed from James Moffatt's terse dictum: "Jesus did not preach justification; Paul did"!)[4]

The actual word "justified" appears in the parable of the Pharisee and the tax-collector. The tax-collector, acknowledging that he was a sinner and casting himself on God's grace, "went down to his house justified rather than the other" (Luke 18:14a). Professor Jeremias argues that in this last phrase Luke is not taking over a Pauline expression, because "justified rather than the other" reflects a Semitic idiom which plays no part in Paul's formulations of the doctrine. The Lukan passage, he thinks, "has the priority: Jesus was the first to designate the acceptance of the sinner by God as *dikaiousthai,* i.e., as an anticipated eschatological acquittal."[5]

More important than the actual word, however, is the reality which it expresses. Of the cleansing of the leper in Mark 1:40-45, for example, Alan Richardson says that "the whole Pauline doctrine of justification 'by faith is expounded in this short *pericope,* which carries us to the very heart of the Gospel message of forgiveness."[6] For, he says, by touching the leper and so taking on Himself the burden of defilement, Jesus reveals Himself as the sin-bearer. In working out the significance of the details of this incident, Dr. Richardson has overdone their allegorization, but the central point which he makes is clear enough.

Again, the last-hired workmen in the parable of the laborers in the vineyard do not bargain with the owner about their pay (Matt. 20:1-16). If a denarius was the fair rate for a day's work, those who worked for the last hour only might have expected but a small fraction of that, but they accepted the owner's undertaking to give them "whatever is right," and in the event they too received a denarius each. As T. W. Manson remarks: "God's love cannot be portioned out in quantities nicely adjusted to the merits of individuals. There is such a thing as the twelfth part of a denar. It was called a *pondion.* But there is no such thing as a twelfth part of the love of God."[7]

The same principle appears in the parable of the two debtors. One owed a large sum and the other a small sum, but neither

4. "Paul and Jesus," *Biblical World* 32 (1908), pp. 168ff., quoted by V. P. Furnish, *Bulletin of the John Rylands Library* 47, p. 356.

5. *Expository Times* 66, p. 369.

6. *The Miracle Stories of the Gospels* (London, 1941), p. 61.

7. *The Sayings of Jesus* (London, 1949), p. 220.

could repay what he owed, and so the creditor, in the noble phrase of the King James Version, "frankly forgave them both" (Luke 7:42).

We see it again in the parable of the prodigal son (Luke 15:11-32). When the black sheep of the family came home in disgrace and started off with the fine speech he had so carefully rehearsed, his father might easily have said: "That's all very well, young man; we have heard fine speeches before. Now you buckle to and work as you have never worked in your life, and if we see that you really mean what you say, we may let you work your passage. But first you must prove yourself; we can't let bygones be bygones as though nothing had happened." Even that would have done the young man a world of good, and even the elder brother might have consented to let him be placed on probation. And that is very much like some people's idea of God. But it was not Jesus' way of presenting God—nor was it Paul's.

For—and here is where the Pauline doctrine of justification comes in—God does not treat us like that. He does not put us on probation to see how we shall turn out—although, if He did so, that in itself would be an act of grace. But then we should never be really satisfied that we had made the grade, that our performance was sufficiently creditable to win the divine approval at the last. Even if we did the best we could—and somehow we do not always manage to do that—how could we be sure that our best came within measurable distance of God's requirement? We might hope, but we could never be certain. But if God in sheer grace assures us of our acceptance in advance, and we gladly embrace that assurance, then we can go on to do His will from the heart as our response of love, without constantly worrying whether we are doing it adequately or not. In fact, to the end of the chapter we shall be unprofitable servants, but we know whom we have believed:

> He owns me for His child;
> I can no longer fear.

And how can such grace be accepted save by childlike trust, grateful faith? For Paul, as for Jesus, "religion is grace and ethics is gratitude."[8]

The initiative in grace always rests with God. He bestows the reconciliation; men receive it (Rom. 5:11). In Paul's thought,

---

8. T. Erskine, *Letters* (Edinburgh, 1877), p. 16.

"God, who through Christ reconciled us to himself" (II Cor. 5:18), no more needs to be Himself reconciled than the father in the parable needed to be reconciled to his returning son. It was the son's heart, not the father's, that had to undergo a change.

So also God provides the redemption; men are its beneficiaries. The "redemption (*apolytrōsis*) which is in Christ Jesus" (Rom. 3:24) was spoken of in advance by Jesus when He said that the Son of Man came "not to receive service but to give it, and to give his life a ransom (*lytron*) for many" (Mark 10:45).

This subject of the affinity between Paul's doctrine of justification and the central emphasis in Jesus' teaching is explored in depth by Eberhard Jüngel in his *Paulus und Jesus*—a book described in its subtitle as "an inquiry into the more precise formulation of the question of the origin of Christology." Jüngel is a pupil of Ernst Fuchs, a distinguished member of the Bultmann schoool, and he pays tribute to Bultmann by endorsing the judgment that "in the past generation of New Testament scholars no-one, apart from Schlatter, has done so much as Bultmann for the recovery of the Reformers' doctrine of justification."[9] His procedure is to examine first the outlines of Paul's doctrine of justification, then the outlines of the message of Jesus, and lastly the relation between the two. "The eschatological character both of Jesus' proclamation and of Paul's doctrine of justification enables us to make a positive comparison of the two lines of teaching one with the other":[10] on this score he is at one with Albert Schweitzer, although he is far from accepting Schweitzer's attitude to New Testament eschatology.

Jesus' proclamation of the kingdom of God is studied in the parables; Jüngel insists repeatedly that in the parables the kingdom of God comes to expression, and that the hearers' response to the parables is their response to the kingdom of God. Jesus' parabolic teaching is more than mere teaching: it is a *Sprachereignis,* a "speech-event" or "language-event," in the sense that the parabolic teaching is itself an event confronting the hearer and challenging him to say "Yes" to the demand of the kingdom of God. With Fuchs, Jüngel sees in the parables Jesus' christological testimony to Himself, albeit in veiled form.

During the ministry, Jesus' conduct and attitude supplied a

9. *Paulus und Jesus* (Tübingen, 1962), p. 24.
10. Ibid., p. 266.

sufficient commentary for understanding the parables; later, the church felt it necessary to supply its own verbal commentary. In the "Son of Man" sayings Jüngel discerns the same eschatological note as in the parables. It is this eschatological note which he hears sounding in Paul's teaching on justification and providing the link between Paul and Jesus. "Christ is the end (*telos*) of the law for every believer" (Rom. 10:4) because in Him the *eschaton* has arrived; Christ as the end of the law is accordingly the ground of men's justification before God. (He interprets Paul's *telos* in the sense of the *eschaton,* the last thing of all—or perhaps it would be better to say that he interprets the *eschaton* as having already been realized in Christ's definitive work.) In the preaching of Jesus and the teaching of Paul, he finds the same relation between eschatology and history, the same emphasis on the end of the law, the same demand for faith —the faith that works by love. The difference lies simply in this, that the *eschaton* which for Jesus lay in the near future, is present for Paul.

It would be more accurate to say that, for Paul, the age in which he was living was not yet the *telos* (cf. I Cor. 15:24) or the *eschaton,* but its threshold, the time of the messianic birth pangs, by means of which the new creation was coming into life through the gospel. Paul's desire was to absorb these birth pangs as completely as possible in his own experience, so that his fellow believers would have the less to endure. But here and now the presence and power of the Spirit in their lives provided the anticipation—in Paul's words, the "earnest," "first fruits" or "seal"—of that heritage of glory which would be theirs at the final emergence of the new creation and disappearance of the old.

The actions of Jesus, as well as His parables, come into view here. The parables we have considered were mostly told to underline the special welcome that God reserves for the rejects of society, the outcasts, the wholesale sinners, the Gentiles. And Jesus brought home this attitude of God by extending just such a special welcome to people like these. For this He incurred the reproach of the pious and the orthodox, just as Paul did by extending the blessings of the kingdom of God to Gentiles, and to *such* Gentiles—the untutored idolaters of Lycaonia, the outrageous libertines of Corinth—in the name of that God who "justifies the ungodly" (Rom. 4:5).

Like his Master before him, Paul was a great breaker-down of barriers. This is how Ernst Käsemann puts it:

Paul's doctrine of justification, with the doctrine of the law that belongs to it, is ultimately his interpretation of Christology. It proclaims the "true God and true man" in its way by expressing the fact that the true God joins himself to the ungodly and brings them salvation, as he did through Jesus—the ungodly, but not the Pharisees, the Zealots or the men of Qumran. It proclaims true man by depicting the One who is intolerable to the good people of his time, the One who breaks through their taboos and can only die for them. The Pauline doctrine of justification is entirely and solely Christology, a Christology, indeed, won from Jesus' cross and hence an offensive Christology. Its point is the *ecce homo* presented so that we, confronted with the Nazarene, learn how little our illusions about ourselves and the world can stand up to his reality. But it is this which is the breakthrough to the new creation.[11]

Professor Käsemann (characteristically) exaggerates at several points for (as usual) he is polemicizing. The Pharisees, Zealots, and men of Qumran were not excluded from the Father's house save insofar as, like the elder brother, they excluded themselves. But even if he exaggerates, the point he so emphasizes is the center of the gospel, Jesus' gospel—and Paul's.

It is not surprising that scholars in the Lutheran tradition should concentrate in this way on Paul's teaching about justification by faith and its links with the ministry of Jesus; but similar conclusions could be reached if the same kind of attention were directed towards other dominant themes of Paul's teaching.

The Father and the Spirit

That Jesus' term for God, Abba, had found its way into the language of Greek-speaking Christians before Paul's mission, or at least independently of it, appears from Paul's assumption that it is known in the Roman church, which he had never visited (Rom. 8:15), as well as in the churches of Galatia which he himself planted (Gal. 4:6). But the manner in which Paul grasped the fundamental importance of Jesus' teaching about the Fatherhood of God, and linked it to his own teaching about the Spirit, is plain from his insistence that "the Spirit of adoption" by whose impulsion the children of God are prompted to address Him spontaneously as "Abba Father" is no other than

---

11. *Perspectives on Paul* (London, 1971), p. 73.

"the Spirit of his Son"—the Spirit that indwelt and animated Jesus. And, according to Paul, to be led by this Spirit is the very principle of the freedom of the Christian life: "if you are led by the Spirit, you are not under law" (Gal. 5:18).

Salvation-History

The relation of Paul and Jesus in respect of salvation-history is another matter that calls for attention.

Salvation-history (a rendering of the more compact German compound *Heilsgeschichte*) presents the saving activity of God in historical terms: it envisages a process characterized by preparation and accomplishment, by promise and fulfillment, by challenge and response, in which the pattern of the saving activity is reproduced repeatedly until it reaches its culmination in the redemptive work of Christ. It is marked by teleology, by the tracing of one increasing purpose to be consummated in the fullness of time. This, as we have seen in Chapter 2, is exactly the motif of Ephesians 1:9f. In fact this is one of the reasons for which the Pauline authorship of Ephesians is questioned by those who believe Paul to have been free from this salvation-history perspective.

This viewpoint is particularly common among members of the Bultmann school who treat the salvation-history perspective as a deviation from the true gospel (existentially interpreted) and as a symptom of "incipient catholicism" (*Frühkatholizismus*) and deprecate it as an attempt to find an adventitious security in place of that challenge to enter authentic existence which is, in their estimate, the heart of the gospel. That the salvation-history perspective is present in Ephesians, and still more emphatically in the writings of Luke, is agreed;[12] any suggestion that it is present in the "capital" Pauline letters tends to be resisted or minimized.

The Paul of Acts certainly thinks and speaks in terms of salvation-history, not only in his synagogue address at Pisidian Antioch (Acts 13:16-41) but also in his speech to the Court of the Areopagus at Athens (Acts 17:22-31). This latter speech, in the words of Professor Hans Conzelmann, "takes world history as one of its themes," embracing "the ideas of the Creation (the past), of God's dominion over the world (the present) and

---

12. Cf. E. Käsemann, "Ephesians and Acts," *Studies in Luke-Acts,* ed. L. E. Keck and J. L. Martyn (Nashville, 1966), pp. 288ff.

of the Judgment (the future).[13] The assertion that the coming of Jesus marks the end of the era of God's overlooking men's ignorance of his nature, with the attendant summons to repentance, is underlined by being set in a framework of universal history. The interval preceding the day of judgment is no long one; the certainty of its imminence enforces the summons to repentance. But, for those who see salvation-history as something alien to Paul's thought, the presence of this framework in itself provides sufficient evidence that the Areopagus speech is essentially Lukan and non-Pauline.

But the Paul of the "capital" letters also reveals a salvation-history pattern, although his understanding of it is controlled by the centrality of justification by faith in his thinking. In Galatians 4:4f., for example, he insists that it was in "the fullness of time" that "God sent his Son, born of woman, born under law, to redeem those who were under the law, so that we might receive adoption as sons."[14] The "fullness of time" means that the law had run its course, and was now to be superseded by the age of the Spirit, inaugurated by the accomplishment of Christ's redemptive work. The people of God, according to Paul, had now emerged from their infancy, during which they were under the tutelage of the law; they had come of age, and were called to exercise their responsible liberty as God's freeborn and full-grown sons. "Because you are sons, God has sent the Spirit of his Son into our hearts, . . . so through God you are no longer a slave but a son" (Gal. 4:6f.). When the returning prodigal planned to say to his father, "treat me as one of your hired servants," his father spoke of him as "this my son" (Luke 15:19, 24). We recall, too, how John Wesley in later years looked back on what is commonly called his conversion as the occasion when he exchanged the faith of a servant for the faith of a son.

As Paul viewed the course of sacred history, the age of law was a parenthesis in the record of God's dealings with His people —one which broke into, although it did not suspend, the operation of God's saving grace. For, long before the law was given through Moses, God's saving grace was revealed in the promise to Abraham and his offspring: "In you shall all the nations be blessed" (Gal. 3:8, quoting Gen. 12:3). In receiving this promise Abraham (according to Paul) had the gospel preached to him in advance, and in believing the promise Abraham became the

---

13. *The Theology of Saint Luke* (London, 1960), p. 168; cf. "The Address of Paul on the Areopagus," *Studies in Luke-Acts*, pp. 217ff.

14. See p. 21.

prototype of all who were thereafter to believe the gospel and
have their faith counted to them for righteousness. In Christ,
who is Himself Abraham's offspring, the promise is fulfilled; in
Christ believers receive the inheritance of which the promise
spoke, and of which the present impartation of the Spirit is the
initial pledge.

Again, in I Corinthians 15:20-28, Paul shows how with the
death and resurrection of Christ the parenthetic age of law
has been superseded by the "days of the Messiah." From His
place of enthronement at God's right hand the Messiah is now
reigning until all His enemies have been subdued. With the sub-
duing of death, the last of these enemies, the "days of the
Messiah" will be completed and the resurrection age will be
ushered in.

Earlier in the same letter the presentation of Christ as "our
passover" (I Cor. 5:7f.) and the typological treatment of the
exodus and wilderness narratives (I Cor. 10:1-11) exhibit the
features of salvation-history. The parallel between the earlier
experiences of Israel and the New Testament phase of the
existence of the people of God is but one instance of the tracing
of a recurrent pattern of divine action and human response which
was well established in primitive Christianity and which appears
independently in a number of New Testament documents.

Nowhere does Paul expound salvation-history more fully than
in his letter to the Romans. Not once only but in several ways
this letter presents the salvation of God in a historical setting.
Its opening sentence declares, among other things, that "the
gospel of God" was "promised beforehand through his prophets
in the holy scriptures" and that Jesus "was descended from
David according to the flesh," while He was "designated Son of
God in power according to the Spirit of holiness by his resurrection from the dead" (1:1-4). The outline in Romans 1:18-32
of the progressive revealing of divine retribution against the
sin of mankind, Gentiles and Jews alike, forms the background
to the revealing of divine grace in the gospel. The portrayal of
Abraham as the archetypal man of faith, briefly sketched in
Galatians 3:6ff., is elaborated in Romans 4:1-25. The holy land
which was promised to Abraham and his offspring is now expanded to take in the whole world, which through the gospel is
accepting the kingship of Christ. But the central blessing of the
promise to Abraham—justification by faith—is not deferred to
the time of the ultimate fulfillment of the promise: as Abraham
received it on the spot when he believed God, so it is received

on the spot by those in any generation who similarly take God at His word.

Again, in Romans 5:12-21 the Adam-Christ antithesis is presented in the form of salvation-history. Adam is the solidarity of unregenerate mankind, destined to be dissolved and replaced by the solidarity of the new creation in Christ. For Paul, Adam, head of the old humanity, is as much a historical figure as Christ, head of the new humanity. He traces the time sequence (i) from Adam to Moses, during which sin was present in latent form, even in the absence of explicit law; (ii) from Moses to Christ, during which latent sin was forced into the open and made to multiply under the action of explicit law; followed by (iii) the new age inaugurated by Christ, into which His followers have entered and in which grace reigns in place of law. But Adam and Christ, the two poles of this course of history, are at the same time present realities, and the gospel challenges man in Adam with the call to enter into real life in Christ.

The recognition of this existential challenge makes good those defects which have been found in a purely salvation-history approach to Paul. The challenge to decision can come, and the response of faith can be made, at any point along the line. The work of Christ has been uniquely effective in pointing the challenge and eliciting the faith: the "now" of II Corinthians 6:2, "*now* is the acceptable time, . . . *now* is the day of salvation," is the "*now*" of Acts 17:30f.: "God *now* commands all men everywhere to repent, because he has fixed a day on which he will judge the world in righteousness by a man whom he has appointed, and of this he has given assurance to all men by raising him from the dead."

For Paul, then, salvation-history was no mere theological scheme, intellectually constructed; it was the redemptive action of God in which Paul knew himself to be personally and totally involved—first as its beneficiary, when the risen Lord apprehended him, and then as its herald among the Gentiles. Salvation-history is present in Paul as surely as in Luke, but Paul sets it in a perspective which is peculiarly his own.

The note of present urgency in Paul's "*now* is the acceptable time" is struck in the teaching of Jesus in the Gospels: "Today this scripture has been fulfilled in your hearing," He said (Luke 4:21) with reference to the proclamation of "the acceptable year of the Lord" in Isaiah 61:2. And if it be objected that the record of Jesus' preaching at Nazareth (Luke 4:16ff.) is really an expression of Luke's salvation-history, the answer is that there is ample evidence, outside Luke's special material, of a salvation-history element in the preaching of Jesus.

The proclamation of the kingdom of God in itself involves a salvation-history perspective. The very term "the kingdom of God" cannot be understood apart from its Old Testament background, and in particular from the announcement in Daniel 2:44 that, when Gentile world-power has run its course, "the God of heaven will set up a kingdom which shall never be destroyed, . . . and it will stand for ever." This kingdom is to be entrusted, when the appointed time comes, to "the saints of the Most High" (Dan. 7:18, 22, 27). So when Jesus, on the morrow of John the Baptist's arrest, began to proclaim in Galilee that the appointed time had been fulfilled and the kingdom of God had drawn near,[15] and called on His hearers to repent and believe this good news, His words would have been taken to mean that the climax of history was at hand and that the eternal kingdom foreseen by Daniel was about to be established. His was not the only voice in Israel at that time to proclaim the imminence of the kingdom of God, but His understanding of the nature of that kingdom differed radically from the most popular view. The Zealots, whose calculations led them to the conclusion that "at that very time"[16] world dominion would be achieved by Israel, believed it their duty to promote the fulfillment of the divine purpose by militant violence against the pagan empire. For Jesus, the fulfillment of the divine purpose and the establishment of the new age depended on the triumph through suffering of Daniel's "one like a son of man" (7:13), which He knew Himself called to fulfill. When He assured His disciples that, "little flock" as they might be in comparison with the big battalions of the day, it was the Father's purpose to give them the kingdom (Luke 12:32), He marked them out as the "saints of the Most High" who were to receive the kingdom, in fellowship with the Son of Man. Indeed, the whole process of sacred history led up to the situation in which His disciples now found themselves: "Blessed are your eyes, for they see, and your ears, for they hear. Truly, I say to you, many prophets and righteous men longed to see what you see, and did not see it; and to hear what you hear, and did not hear it" (Matt. 13:16f.; cf. Luke 10:23f.).

The establishment of the kingdom would be attended by a

---

15. See p. 21.

16. Tacitus, *Histories* v. 13; similar language is used by Josephus (*War* vi. 312) and Suetonius (*Vespasian* 4. 5).

crisis which would overwhelm with disaster those who were not prepared to meet it, as surely as Noah's deluge and the destruction of the cities of the plain overwhelmed those who refused to be warned in time. Between the period of the ministry ("already") and the consummation of the kingdom ("not yet") Jesus foresaw an interval of indeterminate duration, introduced by the rejection and passion of the Son of Man, apart from which the kingdom could not come "with power" (Mark 9:1; cf. 13:10). It is widely held that those parables which presuppose a delay in the glorious advent of the Son of Man reflect the situation a generation or more after the ministry, when His advent, originally expected immediately, had actually been delayed. But to hold this is to assume in advance that the advent in Jesus' authentic teaching is invariably to be expected immediately.

Jesus not only viewed His ministry as inaugurating the accomplishment of the divine purpose for the world, towards which all past time had been moving forward, but He viewed Himself as the key figure and agent in bringing about the culmination of salvation-history. The preachers and theologians of the primitive church, according to their varying perspectives as the sequel to Jesus' ministry unfolded itself, were concerned to develop and re-interpret an understanding of salvation-history which came to expression in Jesus Himself. Pre-eminent among these was Paul. As in Paul, salvation-history is the "sphere" of the justifying grace of God, so in Jesus it is the "sphere" of the Father's pardoning love portrayed in His parables, and, above all, in His own friendly and unaffected welcome to outcasts and sinners.

When W. G. Kümmel gave his presidential address in 1963 to the Society for New Testament Studies on Jesus and Paul, he concluded with words which may aptly be quoted as summarizing the substance of this chapter.

> The reality *and* the proclamation of God's eschatological salvation—a salvation already being realized and to be consummated in the near future—have their roots in Jesus himself, and Paul is but the herald of this reality in the new situation created by God in the church of the Risen One. We cannot choose between Jesus and Paul; all that we can do is in Paul's witness to encounter Jesus himself, who is the ground and the truth of this witness.[17]

---

17. "Jesus und Paulus," *New Testament Studies* 10 (1963-64), p. 181.

5

The Teaching of Jesus

There has been the widest diversity in assessing the extent of Paul's knowledge of, or dependence on, explicit sayings of Jesus. In 1904 Arnold Resch thought he could recognize allusions to 925 such sayings in nine Pauline letters, with 133 in Ephesians and 100 in the Pastorals, not to mention allusions to dozens of otherwise unrecorded sayings of Jesus.[1] We can all, of course, recognize the source of the reference to "faith that removes mountains" in I Corinthians 13:2, but incidental expressions so unambiguously dominical as this are rare. At the opposite extreme from Resch, Rudolf Bultmann maintains that "the teaching of the historical Jesus plays no role or practically none in Paul . . ."[2]

He quotes "words of the Lord" only at I Cor. 7:10f. and 9:14, and in both uses they are regulations for church life. It is possible that echoes of words of the Lord are present in Paul's parenesis: e.g., Rom. 12:14 (Mt. 5:44); 13:9f. (Mk. 12:31); 16:19 (Mt. 10:16); I Cor. 13:2 (Mk. 11:23). The tradition of the Jerusalem Church is at least in substance behind the "word of the Lord" on the parousia and resurrection in I Thess. 4:15-17, though it is not certain whether Paul is

---

1. *Der Paulinismus und die Logia Jesu—Texte und Untersuchungen, neue Folge* 12 (1904). He also claimed to identify 64 further sayings of Jesus in the Pauline speeches in Acts.
2. *Theology of the New Testament,* i (1952), p. 35; he adds "or John."

here quoting a traditionally transmitted saying or whether he is appealing to a revelation accorded to him by the exalted Lord. But of decisive importance in this connection is the fact that Paul's theology proper . . . is not at all a recapitulation of Jesus' own preaching or a further development of it, and it is especially significant that he never adduces any of the sayings of Jesus on the Torah in favor of his own teaching about the Torah.[3]

"The Word of the Lord"

Professor Bultmann's reference to "the word of the Lord" in I Thessalonians 4:15 has been mentioned above in the discussion of the mystery of the end-time.[4] We cannot be sure whether Paul is quoting a *verbum Christi* which had come down to him by tradition but has not been preserved for us except in this context, or one which was communicated by the risen Lord through a prophet. In either case, it has something of the status of a new revelation, so that in effect it does not differ greatly from the "mystery" which Paul unfolds to the Corinthians on a closely related subject in I Corinthians 15:51, although the word "mystery" is not used in the context of I Thessalonians 4:13. The main distinction would be that the "mystery" was made known in the first instance to Paul himself, whereas the "word of the Lord" was heard by a greater company.

"Eat What Is Set Before You"

But let us take something on a more everyday level than such an oracular pronouncement—an incidental remark in Paul's Corinthian correspondence, in a section where he answers one by one questions addressed to him in a letter from the church of Corinth. The question under discussion is that of eating the flesh of animals which have been offered in sacrifice to pagan divinities. A Christian with conscientious scruples about such food can bar it from his own house, but what is he to do when he is eating out? Plainly this is not a question on which a direct ruling will be found in the teaching of Jesus. The subject arises out of the Gentile mission, which is fraught with technical problems unknown in the setting of the Galilean ministry. What then does Paul say? "If one of the unbelievers invites you to

3. Ibid., pp. 188f.
4. See p. 32.

a dinner and you are disposed to go, eat whatever is set before you (*pan to paratithemenon hymin esthiete*) without raising any question on the ground of conscience" (I Cor. 10:27).

To anyone familiar with the Gospels, some of these words ring a bell. In His instructions to the seventy disciples in Luke 10:8, Jesus says: "Whenever you enter a town and they receive you, eat what is set before you" (*esthiete ta paratithemena hymin*). Is this similarity a mere coincidence, or is Paul echoing a *verbum Christi*? Perhaps he is. What, we may ask, was the force of this injunction in its Gospel context? No such injunction appears in the parallel commission to the twelve, in any of its three versions, whereas in the commission to the seventy it appears twice, albeit in different terms (cf. Luke 10:7, "remain in the same house, eating and drinking what they provide"). But the mission of the twelve was restricted to Israel, expressly so in Matthew 10:5f. and by implication in Mark 6:7-11 and Luke 9:1-5. The mission of the seventy, on the other hand, which is peculiar to Luke, has commonly been thought to adumbrate the wider Gentile mission which he records in his second volume. Whereas twelve was the number of the tribes of Israel, seventy was in Jewish tradition the conventional number of the nations of the world. (If we adopted the variant reading "seventy-two" instead of "seventy" in Luke 10:1, 17, the situation would be rather different.)

If, then, Paul in I Corinthians 10:27 is quoting from Jesus' instructions to the seventy, he is generalizing from a particular occasion to a recurring situation. That he is indeed quoting from these instructions is rendered the more probable because of his allusions, in the same context, to another part of the same commission. In I Corinthians 9:1-27 he interrupts his discussion of food offered to idols, where he has said that in certain circumstances he places voluntary restrictions on his undoubted Christian liberty, to enlarge on the subject of such self-imposed restrictions in one special matter which was misunderstood, and indeed misrepresented, in the Corinthian church.

"The Laborer Deserves His Wages"

The members of that church could not understand why Paul would not accept financial support from them, when, as they knew, he accepted it from other churches. One reason for his policy seems to have been that there was so much opposition to him at Corinth, whether generated within the church or imported from outside, that he suspected that his acceptance of money from that church would give his traducers an opportunity to accuse him of mercenary motives. Since he made it his business to give them no such opportunity, they represented this as evidence of his inner awareness that he was not an apostle in the full sense of the word and therefore not entitled to the right of which Peter and his colleagues, together with members of the family of Jesus, availed themselves, of living at the expense of their converts and others for whose spiritual well-being they cared. He replies that he is indeed an apostle in the fullest sense, as the Corinthian Christians well know, and that he certainly has the right of living at their expense, but exercises his liberty of choice by refusing to avail himself of that right. That it is indeed a right he argues on the basis of natural law and divine law, but supremely on the ground that none less than "the Lord commanded that those who proclaim the gospel should get their living by the gospel' (I Cor. 9:14). This command does not appear expressly in any of our canonical Gospels, but it is to the same effect as a principle which is enunciated in two slightly different forms in the Matthean commission to the twelve (10:10), "the laborer deserves his food" (trophē), and in the Lukan commission to the seventy (10:7), "the laborer deserves his wages" (misthos). Of these two forms, it is the latter that comes closer to the sense that Paul has in mind. It is nowhere suggested that he would decline to accept *food* in the home of one of his Corinthian friends, whether it were "Gaius my host" (Rom. 16:23) or anyone else. It was not food but *wages,* monetary payment, that he would not take from them, even if he asserts his right to accept it, or even require it, if he so chose. (We note further that, when the same subject is taken up later in I Timothy 5:17f. and applied to the material support of elders in a local church, the Lukan form of the saying, "the laborer deserves his wages," is quoted *verbatim.*)

In his valuable study of *The Sayings of Jesus in the Churches of Paul,* David Dungan devotes a good deal of space to discussing why Paul, in quoting this command of the Lord, nevertheless (as he makes plain in the context) deliberately disobeys it. He concludes that Paul either "initially turned this regulation into a permission" of which he was free to avail himself or not, if indeed he had not "simply inherited this alteration ready-made." One way or the other "this alteration is based on the realization that this regulation was no longer appropriate in every case."[5]

But I must confess that it never occurred to me that the "command" was not essentially intended as a permission from the outset. It is provided by Act of Parliament in the United Kingdom that members of the House of Commons shall be paid annually a certain sum of money, consisting partly of taxable income and partly of an expense allowance. The withholding of this payment from a member of the House without due cause would certainly be a breach of the law. But no law compels a member, or could compel him, to *accept* payment. Whether he accepts the payment to which he is entitled or not lies within his free choice, and so it was with Paul.

Paul, of course, had been brought up to believe that the teaching of the Torah should not be treated as a means of livelihood or personal aggrandizement. "He who makes a worldly use of the crown of the Torah will waste away," Hillel had said;[6] and so Paul, pupil of Hillel's most illustrious disciple, was by manual occupation a tent-maker. But he claimed for others the right which he chose to decline for himself: "Let him who is taught the word share all good things with him who teaches" (Gal. 6:6).

In this connection it may be observed that Hillel's dictum is very much in line with an injunction contained in the Matthean commission to the twelve: "Freely you have received; freely give"—or, as RSV renders it, "You received without pay, give without pay" (10:8). Had Paul known this injunction, he might have quoted it to justify his own policy; but whether he knew it or not, he does not quote it.

Divorce

Another dominical ruling which Paul quotes as authoritative and as an end to all controversy is his ruling on divorce. "To the married I say," says Paul to the Corinthians, "not I but the Lord, that the wife should not separate (*chōristhēnai*) from her husband (but if she does, let her remain single or else be reconciled to her husband)— and that the husband should not divorce his wife" (I Cor. 7:10f.).

---

5. *The Sayings of Jesus in the Churches of Paul* (Oxford, 1971), p. 32.

6. *Pirqē Aboth* 1:13; 4:7 (the latter passage quotes also the similar dictum of Rabbi Zadok, "Make not of the Torah a crown wherewith to magnify thyself or a spade wherewith to dig," and from the two quotations the inference is drawn: "Whosoever derives a profit for himself from the words of the Torah is helping on his own destruction").

This is not a *verbatim* quotation—Paul reproduces it in indirect speech, but its relation to the Lord's words in Mark 10:2ff. is fairly plain. When Jesus was asked by the Pharisees whether it was lawful for a man to divorce his wife, he appealed from Moses' concession in Deuteronomy 24:1-4 back to the record of the original creation of man and the institution of marriage in Genesis 1:27 and 2:24 and made the pronouncement: "What therefore God has joined together, let not man put asunder" (*chōrizein*).

What Paul echoes, however, is the more explicit reply made by Jesus in sequel to His disciples' request for a fuller explanation: "Whoever divorces his wife and marries another, commits adultery against her; and if she divorces her husband and marries another, *she* commits adultery" (Mark 10:11f.). Since under Jewish law the husband alone had the right to initiate divorce proceedings, it is frequently supposed that the added words about the wife's taking the initiative represent an extension of the basic principle to the circumstances of the Gentile mission. But we should bear in mind that at the time of Jesus' ministry there had recently been a notorious case of a wife's divorcing her husband and marrying another, in Herodias leaving her first husband to become the wife of his half-brother, Herod Antipas, with whom she now lived in the neighboring city of Tiberias. Herodias, like all the members of the Herod family, was a Roman citizen and could divorce her husband under Roman law, but the whole business was a scandal in the eyes of pious Jews, even if they did not all speak out so plainly about it as John the Baptist had dared to do. It may be observed further that Jesus' ruling, while primarily given as an interpretation of Scripture, had the incidental effect of correcting an unequal balance in the interests of Jewish women, who had but little redress against husbands who chose arbitrarily to divorce them. Men, on the other hand, might feel that He was tilting the balance to their *dis*advantage, as is evident from the disciples' reaction in Matthew 19:10, "If such is the case of a man with his wife, it is not expedient to marry."

It is interesting that Paul (in the Lord's name) enjoins that the wife should not separate from her husband before he says that the husband should not divorce his wife. Why he should do this is not clear, and we can only surmise that his sequence is dictated by the form in which the Corinthians' question was framed. "Should a Christian wife separate from her husband?" No, she should not; she should go on living with him as his wife.

"But what if she has already separated from him?" (Counselors and others who are asked for advice in such delicate matters of human relations constantly find their task made more difficult because they are confronted with *faits accomplis.*) Then let her remain single (*agamos*), says Paul, or else let her be reconciled to her husband. Presumably she separated from her husband because she acquired a distaste for married life (or at least for married life with him). But if she finds the consequent abstention burdensome, it is out of the question for her to marry someone else; let her be reconciled to her lawful husband. We cannot, of course, be sure that this is a correct reconstruction of the background to the Corinthians' question and the apostle's answer; but something of the sort is quite likely. Having dealt with that aspect of the question which was perhaps uppermost in the Corinthians' letter, Paul then adds what was the substantive element in Jesus' ruling: the husband must not divorce his wife.

Paul makes no reference to the exceptive clause, "except for fornication," which appears twice in slightly different wording in Matthew's Gospel (5:32; 19:9). Instead, he introduces an exceptive case on his own initiative: "I say, not the Lord," that if an unbelieving marriage partner is willing to go on living with a husband or wife who has been converted to Christianity, good and well; but the unbeliever who insists on breaking up the marriage must be allowed to go. Some Corinthians may have felt that if one partner only became a Christian he or she would be contaminated by marital relations with the non-Christian spouse. On the contrary, says Paul, the unbeliever is "sanctified" by association with the believer, and the same holds good for their children. And where the two continue happily in married life together, the believing partner may well be the salvation of the other. But where the unbelieving partner refuses to go on with the believer and walks out, in *that* case the marriage bond is no longer binding; the marriage has ceased to exist (I Cor. 7:12-16). I suspect, though it is impossible to put it more positively, that Paul himself had undergone such an experience: if so, he considered himself thereafter to be celibate (*agamos*).

Although no dominical precedent is invoked for this "Pauline privilege," it is plain that Paul did not consider that his concession cut across the Lord's ruling. Rather, the Gentile mission raised practical issues which lay outside the Palestinian situation in which the Pharisees asked their question and Jesus answered it. While remaining faithful to the spirit and principle of

Jesus' answer, Paul had to deal with these new issues as a wise pastor, having regard to the best interests of the people concerned and the public reputation of the Christian community. In this, we may consider, he has left an example for Christian leaders in later centuries, who may find themselves consulted on practical issues, in this or other areas of life, which even Paul never contemplated.

Tribute to Caesar

Jesus' ruling on divorce was given in response to a question which (according to Mark) was designed in some way to catch him out: "Pharisees came up and in order to test him asked, 'Is it lawful for a man to divorce his wife?'" (Mark 10:2). If the Pharisees on this occasion were accompanied by Herodians, as in Mark 3:6, it would not be surprising. A similar preamble introduces the question about tribute money in Mark 12:13ff., in which the Pharisees and Herodians act together: "they sent to him some of the Pharisees, and some of the Herodians, to entrap him in his talk."

Paul deals with the payment of tribute in the much-debated paragraph at the beginning of Romans 13 (vv. 1-7), but there he does not invoke the Lord's authority as he does in I Corinthians 9:14 or 7:10. Moreover, whereas Jesus draws a contrast between rendering to Caesar what is Caesar's and rendering to God what is God's, Paul sees in the rendering of Caesar's dues to Caesar one form of rendering to God what God requires, for the secular authorities are God's ministers, and resistance to them involves resistance to God. Therefore, he says, "pay all of them their dues, taxes to whom taxes are due, revenue to whom revenue is due" (Rom. 13:7).

Can we then suppose that, behind Paul's ruling here, Jesus' answer to the question about tribute is to be discerned? Did Paul himself have it at the back of his mind?

Probably he did: "render (*apodote*) to all their dues" (Rom. 13:7) could be a generalization of Mark 12:17, "render (*apodote*) to Caesar what is Caesar's and to God what is God's." But the generalization goes much further. Paul answers the question, "Should Christians in Rome and the Roman Empire, subjects of the emperor, render obedience and tribute to him and to his subordinate officials?" His answer is "Yes, for they rule by God's appointment, and they perform God's service when they maintain law and order, protecting those who do good and executing judgment against wrongdoers." The field of reference is quite different from that with which Jesus had to reckon in Judea, where the rising of Judas the Galilean in A.D. 6 and the Zealot movement which perpetuated its ideals insisted that it was high treason against the God of Israel for His people in His land to acknowledge a pagan monarch by paying him tribute. No such dilemma confronted Paul as that on which Jesus' interlocutors had hoped to impale Him: to Paul the issue was clear, and his own apostolic career had given him repeated opportunities of appreciating the blessings of Roman rule. He was not so naive as to imagine that the higher powers could never act in a manner contrary to the divine ordinance, to a point where Christians would be bound to refuse obedience to them, although he does not raise that issue here. But even here he makes it plain that the duty of obedience to the secular authorities is temporary, lasting only to the end of the present "night"; in the "day" which is "at hand" a new order will be introduced in which "the saints will judge the world" (Rom. 13:12; I Cor. 6:2). The state as we know it is to wither away (here Paul and Karl Marx are in agreement); "the city of God remaineth."

The Law of Christ

Paul might have heard in the school of Gamaliel something to the effect that the whole law was comprehended in the commandment of love to one's neighbor—we recall how Gamaliel's master, Hillel, summarized it in the injunction, "Do not to another what is hateful to yourself"[7]—but when he speaks of the bearing of one another's burdens as the fulfillment of "the law of Christ" (Gal. 6:2), it is a reasonable inference that he knew of the way in which Christ had applied the law of Leviticus 19:18 ("You shall love your neighbor as yourself"). Moreover, the injunction "bear one another's burdens" seems to be a generalizing expansion of Galatians 6:1: "If a man is overtaken in a trespass, you who are spiritual should restore him in a spirit of gentleness." This is strangely reminiscent of a dominical injunction found in Matthew only: "If your brother sins, go and tell him his fault, between you and him alone. If he listens to you, you have gained your brother" (18:15).

Further features of "the law of Christ" may be recognized in Romans 12:9-21, with its injunctions to deep, unaffected, and

7. Babylonian Talmud, tractate *Shabbath,* 31a.

practical love, which are particularly reminiscent of the Sermon on the Mount. Mutual love, sympathy, and honor within the believing brotherhood are to be expected, but this section enjoins, in addition, love and forgiveness towards those outside the brotherhood, not least towards its enemies and persecutors. "Bless those who persecute you; bless and do not curse them" (Rom. 12:14) echoes Luke 6:28: "Bless those who curse you; pray for those who abuse you." So Paul, speaking of his own practice, says, "When reviled, we bless; when persecuted, we endure; when slandered, we try to conciliate (I Cor. 4:12f.).

"Repay no one evil for evil" (Rom. 12:17) breathes the same spirit as Matthew 5:44 and Luke 6:27, "Love your enemies, do good to those who hate you"; and so does the quotation from Proverbs 25:21f. in Romans 12:20. It is probably significant that Paul's quotation leaves out the last clause of the original. "If your enemy is hungry," he says, "feed him; if he is thirsty, give him drink; for by so doing you will heap burning coals upon his head"—but he does not go on to say: "and the Lord will reward you." The "burning coals" may originally have indicated intensified retribution, but whatever the primary force of the injunction may have been, Paul gives it a nobler meaning by placing it in this new context: "Treat your enemy kindly, for this may make him ashamed of his hostile conduct and lead to his repentance." In other words, the best way to get rid of an enemy is to turn him into a friend and so "overcome evil with good" (Rom. 12:21).

The same theme is renewed in Romans 13:8-10, after Paul's words about the duty of Christians to the civil authorities. With reference to the authorities he says, "Pay all of them their dues" (Rom. 13:7), and then continues, more generally: "Let the only debt you owe anyone be the debt of love; the man who has discharged his debt has fulfilled the law." This is supported by the quotation of Leviticus 19:18 ("You shall love your neighbor as yourself") as a summary of all the commandments, which places Paul squarely within the tradition of Jesus. For Jesus set these words alongside those of Deuteronomy 6:5 ("You shall love the Lord your God . . ."), the "great and first commandment," and said: "On these two commandments depend all the law and prophets" (Matt. 22:37-40; Mark 12:28-34). Paul quotes the second great commandment here and not the first because the immediate question concerns a Christian's duty to his neighbor. The commandments in the second table of the decalogue (most of which are quoted in Rom. 13:9) forbid the harming of a neighbor in any way; since love never harms another, "love is the fulfilling of the law" (Rom. 13:10).

When, in the next paragraph (vv. 11-14), Paul goes on to speak of Christian life in days of crisis, he once more echoes the teaching of Jesus. When Jesus spoke of the critical events preceding the coming of the Son of Man, He said to His disciples: "When these things begin to take place, look up and raise your heads, because your redemption is drawing near" (Luke 21:28). Those who hoped "to stand before the Son of Man" must therefore be alert and vigilant (Luke 21:36). "It is full time now," says Paul, "for you to wake from sleep; for salvation is nearer to us now than when we first believed" (Rom. 13:11). The events of the sixties—the imperial persecution of Christians and the Jewish revolt against Rome—were nearer than they had been during the ministry of Jesus. That these events would not be the immediate precursor of the final salvation of all believers was something which Paul could not have foreseen; the knowledge of the decisive day and hour was withheld from the Son of Man himself. But Jesus' words, "he who endures to the end will be saved" (Mark 13:13), verified themselves in the experience of His people who passed through these crises as they have done in other crises. With the affliction comes the way of deliverance. Meanwhile the sons of light must live in readiness for the day of visitation, abjuring all the "works of darkness" (Rom. 13:12).

In another context where Paul deals with the same subject, he tells his readers that since they are sons of light, the day of the Lord, which comes "like a thief in the night," will not take them by surprise (I Thess. 5:2-5). This too takes up a note characteristic of Jesus' teaching: "If the householder had known at what hour the thief was coming, he would have been awake and would not have left his house to be broken into. You also must be ready; for the Son of Man is coming at an hour you do not expect" (Luke 12:39f.; cf. Matt. 24:43f.; Rev. 16:15).[8]

Whereas Paul speaks elsewhere of putting on "the new man" (Eph. 4:24; Col. 3:10), in Romans 13:14 he uses more direct language and bids his readers "put on the Lord Jesus Christ." The Christian graces—making up the "armor of light" which he exhorts them to wear instead of gratifying unregenerate desires —what are they but those graces which were displayed in harmonious perfection in the life and teaching of Jesus?

The practical teaching given to Christian converts in the

---

8. See pp. 32f.

primitive church appears to have been arranged, for easy memorization, under various catchwords, of which "Put on" was one. They were exhorted to "put on" Christian virtues as they would put on new clothes (cf. Col. 3:12), or to "put on" the new character which comprised those virtues, and that new character was the character of the historical Jesus. It was thus an easy transition to say, "as many of you as were baptized into Christ have put on Christ" (Gal. 3:27), or, with the imperative replacing the indicative, "put on the Lord Jesus Christ," to manifest outwardly what they had already experienced inwardly. While Paul did not know the written Gospels as we have them, he knew the qualities which the Evangelists ascribe to Jesus, and commends those qualities, one by one or comprehensively, as an example to his Christian friends.

6

Jesus Is Lord

For Paul the affirmation "Jesus is Lord" is the basic Christian confession. "No one," he maintains, "can say 'Jesus is Lord' except by the Holy Spirit" (I Cor. 12:3).

But to say "Jesus is Lord" in a fully meaningful way requires a positive content for the name "Jesus" as well as for the title "Lord." The affirmation implies that Jesus the crucified (the historical Jesus) has been exalted as Lord.

It has been held, however, that Paul's conception of Jesus as the glorious Lord, a heavenly being, "a lifegiving spirit" (I Cor. 15:45), is incompatible with a genuine acceptance of His historical manhood. This is not so: Paul genuinely accepted the manhood of the One whom he called Lord. There is nothing docetic about his picture of the historical Jesus. However much he does *not* say about Him, he says two things which are incompatible with docetism: Jesus was truly "born of woman" (Gal. 4:4) and as truly suffered death—"the death of the cross" (Phil. 2:8). As these two statements imply, His body was a real "body of flesh" (Col. 1:22). Such expressions as "born in the likeness of man" and "found in human form" (Phil. 2:7f.) should not mislead us; apart from the consideration that they may belong to a pre-Pauline confession there is a high probability that they represent alternative Greek renderings of the Aramaic phrase k*bar-'enâsh* ("like a son of man") in Daniel

81

7:13. As for the Pauline phrase in Romans 8:3, where God is said to have sent His Son "in the likeness of sinful flesh" (lit. "in likeness of flesh of sin"), it is not the noun "flesh" but the adjective "sinful" that demands the addition of "likeness," lest it should be thought that Jesus' human flesh was sinful flesh.

At the same time it is evident that Paul ascribed to Jesus pre-existence and a cosmic role. We acknowledge, he wrote to the Corinthians, "one God, the Father, from whom are all things and unto whom we exist, and one Lord, Jesus Christ, through whom are all things and through whom we exist" (I Cor. 8:6). In II Corinthians 4:4 Christ is "the image of God"; in II Corinthians 8:9 "the grace of our Lord Jesus" is seen in the fact that, though He was rich, yet for His people's sake He became poor, that through His poverty they might become rich—a patent reference to His self-denial in becoming man. This is spelled out in greater detail in Philippians 2:6ff. Whatever may be the origin of this Christological passage, Paul endorses it completely by integrating it with his argument, and thus commits himself to the affirmation that "Christ Jesus" was already "in the form of God" when, refusing to exploit equality with God as a means of self-aggrandizement, He "emptied himself" and took the form of a servant.

Cosmic Wisdom

If we look for Old Testament antecedents to Philippians 2:6ff., we may find them in those passages which speak of the Servant of the Lord and the Son of Man, but those passages do not speak of pre-existence or agency in creation. It is unlikely that Paul was indebted to the *Similitudes of Enoch,* so we need not look to the depiction in that work of the Son of Man who was named in the presence of the Lord of Spirits before the sun or stars were made (I Enoch 48:2f.) It may well be that the author of the *Similitudes* is dependent here on the figure of Wisdom in the Old Testament, and it is to that figure particularly that we should look in our quest for an Old Testament antecedent to the cosmic role of the pre-existent Christ as portrayed by Paul.

We can see from I Corinthians 1:18-31 how readily the idea of Christ as the wisdom of God could come to Paul's mind, even if here it is not in His cosmic role but in His embodiment of the saving message that He is so viewed. While "Christ cruci-fied" is scandalous to Jews and folly to Gentiles, to those who are called, Jews and Gentiles alike, He embodies the power and wisdom of God: to them He has become true "wisdom from God"—righteousness, holiness, and redemption. But if Christ is once acknowledged as the wisdom of God displayed in redemption, the way is open to recognize Him also as the wisdom of God operative in creation.

This becomes specially evident when we consider the statements in Colossians 1:15ff. that Christ is "the image of the invisible God, the first-born of all creation," that "in him all things were created," that "he is before all things and by him all things cohere," that He is the "beginning." We may not be sure if Paul, in the school of Gamaliel, had learned to regard the Torah as "the desirable instrument with which the world was created" (as Akiba was later to put it),[1] but if he did, he did so because Torah was equated with Wisdom, by which it is repeatedly said in the Old Testament Wisdom literature that God brought creation into being, as in Proverbs 3:19:

> The Lord by wisdom has founded the earth;
> By understanding He has stretched out the heavens.

When, as a result of his conversion, the central place which Torah had until then occupied in Paul's thought and life was thenceforth taken by Christ, what more natural than that he should now conceive of Christ not indeed as the "instrument" but as the agent through whom all things were created?

This was the more natural in that Jesus Himself spoke on occasion in the role of the Wisdom of God. It is noteworthy, moreover, that "Wisdom Christology" appears in several strands of New Testament thought, not only in Paul, but also in the Epistle to the Hebrews, the fourth Gospel, and the Revelation of John. We cannot reasonably put its presence in these disparate documents down to Pauline influence. It antedates Paul and the other writers who use it, and if the source on which they all draw is so early, we may well look for it in the words of Jesus Himself.

When in Colossians 1:16 Paul says of Christ that "in him all things were created" and goes on in verse 18 to call Him the "beginning" (*archē*), we shall not be far wrong in concluding that He is, for Paul, the "beginning" in which, according to Genesis 1:1, "God created the heavens and the earth." But why should Paul call Christ the "beginning" in this sense? Because in Proverbs 8:22 Wisdom, personified, speaks of herself as the

---

1. *Pirqē Aboth* 3:18.

beginning of God's way (*rēshīth darkō*). (We may compare the self-description of the risen Christ in Revelation 3:14, at the outset of the letter to the Laodicean church, as "the beginning of the creation of God".)[2] Now that Wisdom is identified with the pre-existent Christ, it is no longer merely personified, as in the Wisdom literature of the Old Testament, but is recognized as a hypostatic entity.

The cosmic role of Christ is not confined to the old creation: in Colossians He who is Lord of the old creation, "head of every principality and power" (2:10), is also Lord of the new creation, "head of his body the church" (1:18). In both creations alike pre-eminence is His. The title "firstborn" is His in both respects: He who is "firstborn of all creation" in the old order (1:15) is also "firstborn from the dead" by resurrection (1:18). In this latter respect He constitutes a new *archē:* now He who as the first "beginning" brought the universe into being is the divine agent in reconciling the universe to God. The fullness (*plērōma*) not only of the divine essence but of the divine activity has taken up residence in Him, operating now for reconciliation as formerly for creation.

When He receives the title "head" in two respects, as "head of every principality and power," and also as "head of his body the church," the word has a much fuller sense in the second title than in the first. In both it marks Him out as the source or origin, but in the latter the church is envisaged as the body of which He is the head in a physiological analogy, controlling and directing it.

The discernment of the Old Testament concept of Wisdom behind this Christology has not, of course, gone unchallenged. On the continent of Europe, and especially in Germany, the prevalent view is that this Christology is based on the gnostic concept of the heavenly man, who submitted for a season to the power of fate in this sublunary world and has now ascended above the circle of the spheres. Ernst Käsemann, who (probably rightly) finds in Colossians 1:15-20 as it now stands a baptismal liturgy, discerns behind it (when the specifically Christian elements are removed) a pre-Christian gnostic hymn based on "the myth of the Archetypal Man who is also the Redeemer,"

---

2. It has been suggested, but not very convincingly, that the companion title in this verse, "the Amen," echoes Hebrew *'āmōn*, "master workman" (?) in Prov. 8:30; cf. J. A. Montgomery, "The Education of the Seer of the Apocalypse," *Journal of Biblical Literature* 45 (1926), pp. 71ff.

who, as his people's pathfinder, "makes a breach in death's domain" and so delivers them from its power. Whereas in the gnostic picture the Archetypal Man is the head of his body the cosmos, in the Christian expansion the risen Lord is the head of His body the church.[3]

The main difficulty with this view is that nowhere have we any positive evidence of this gnostic myth of a revealer-redeemer except under the influence of the Christian story. Attempts to demonstrate its pre-Christian existence in some of the documents recently discovered near Nag Hammadi are of doubtful validity. One of the documents most confidently adduced in this connection—the *Apocalypse of Adam*—shows fairly certain traces of Christian influence in its vocabulary, if not in its mythology.

An objection brought against the wisdom origin of the Christology of Colossians 1:15-20 is that such thoroughly Jewish argumentation would scarcely have been effective against the type of mind that devised the Colossian heresy. But this passage was probably not composed originally as an answer to the Colossian heresy; it is primarily a confession of the supremacy of Christ, perhaps forming part of a baptismal liturgy. Again, the Colossian heresy had a strong element of Judaism in it— Hellenistic Judaism at that—and in Hellenistic Judaism wisdom speculation carved out a course of its own. However late may be the explicit attestation for the rabbinical identifying of *rēshīth* ("beginning") in Genesis 1:1 with wisdom or Torah —it is first ascribed to Hoshaiah in the third century A.D.[4]—a speculatively-minded Hellenistic reader, considering the opening words of the Greek version of the Bible, *en archē* ("in the beginning"), would have been alerted at once by the word *archē*. This word, from the time of the Ionian philosophers of the sixth century B.C., had borne the sense "first principle" or "element."

What then, it would be asked, was this *archē*, this first principle, "in" which God had created the universe? The wisdom literature of the Old Testament provided an immediate and acceptable answer: He created it "in wisdom" (Ps. 104:24). "Wisdom" is therefore the first principle. According to the chief monument of Hellenistic wisdom literature, Wisdom is "the fashioner of all things," as well as being "a breath of the power of God, and a pure emanation of the glory of the Almighty; . . .

---

3. *Essays on New Testament Themes* (London, 1964), pp. 149ff.
4. As quoted in *Midrash Rabba* on Gen. 1:1.

a reflection (*apaugasma*) of eternal light, a spotless mirror of
the working of God, and an image (*eikon*) of His goodness.[5] This
metaphorical language has become personal in the New Testament. Christ, "through whom are all things" (I Cor. 8:6), is
"the image (*eikōn*) of God" (II Cor. 4:4; Col. 1:15) and the
"reflection (*apaugasma*) of His glory" (Heb. 1:3). "Christ," in
the words of C. F. D. Moule, "has become to Christians all that
the Wisdom of God was, according to the Wisdom literature, and
much more."[6]

Sources of the Christian Confession

For Paul, a true believer is a person who confesses that Jesus
is Lord. To every one who makes this confession, believing in his
heart that God raised Jesus from the dead, salvation is assured
(Rom. 10:9). This parallelism between outward confession and
inward faith implies that "Jesus is Lord" and "God has raised
Him from the dead" are two ways of saying the same thing. It
is as the risen one that Jesus is Lord.

Not that Paul would insist on one invariable formula. Any
other expression that served the same purpose would be acceptable, and "Lord" had a variety of synonyms. Thus, in Romans
1:4, where a pre-Pauline confession is perhaps quoted, Jesus in
resurrection is "designated *Son of God* in power." In the quasi-
hymnic passage later in the same letter, mention is made of
"Christ Jesus who died, yes, who was raised from the dead, who is
at the right hand of God, who indeed intercedes for us" (8:34).
Although the title "Lord" does not expressly appear here, this
passage presents the substance of the title as given to Jesus: it
is as the risen and exalted one that Jesus is Lord. (The ascription of an intercessory ministry to the one at God's right hand
may go back, if Old Testament *testimonia* are sought for it, to
a combination of Isaiah 53:12, where the Servant makes "inter-
cession for the transgressors," with Psalm 110:1, where God
invites His anointed One to sit at His right hand, and Daniel
7:13f., where "one like a Son of Man" is presented before the
Ancient of Days to receive universal and eternal sovereignty—
a combination so primitive that an original setting in the context of Jesus' earthly ministry cannot be excluded.)

In Philippians 2:9-11, similarly, the bestowal on the crucified

---

5. Wisdom 7:22, 25f.
6. *The Epistles to the Colossians and to Philemon* (Cambridge, 1957),
p. 86.

Jesus of the supreme title "Lord" is the climax of His high exaltation by God. In fact, the evidence of all strata of New Testament teaching, and not only of the Pauline writings, leads to the conclusion that the title "Lord" belongs to Jesus as the one whom God has raised from the dead and enthroned alongside Himself.

It has recently been argued, pre-eminently by Ferdinand Hahn of Mainz,[7] that although the title "Lord" in the New Testament writings is overwhelmingly associated with the exaltation of Jesus, it was originally associated with His imminent parousia or advent. But if we look for evidence of this alleged shift from the earlier association of the title with the parousia to its association with Jesus' exaltation, we shall have to date it very early indeed. The Lordship of Jesus is associated with His exaltation and session at God's right hand in the earliest accessible confessional formulae—Romans 8:34 and I Peter 3:22 will serve as examples. (Whatever the date of these letters may be, the confessional language which they quote is still earlier and common Christian property.) If Psalm 110:1 played the part commonly ascribed to it in connection with the invocation of Jesus as Lord, it could not be otherwise; for it is at one and the same time the *testimonium* for His Lordship and for His session at God's right hand. True, the *testimonium* also points on to the consummation, "till I make your enemies your footstool"—but in the New Testament it is frequently quoted without this addendum, and in the places where the addendum is quoted, only once is it expounded (I Cor. 15:25-28).

It cannot be proved—it cannot even be rendered probable—that the present intercessory ministry of the exalted Christ was not envisaged from the first. Stephen's vision of the Son of Man standing at God's right hand comes indeed in a Hellenistic section of Acts, but the title "Son of Man" (here only in the New Testament occurring outside the Gospels) is strikingly un-Hellenistic. Moreover, Stephen's words chime in impressively with the dominical logion of Luke 12:8, "whoever acknowledges me before men will be acknowledged by the Son of Man before the angels of God"—a logion with peculiar claims to be recognized as an *ipsissimum verbum Christi*.

Those who envisage a shift from the earlier association of Jesus' Lordship with His coming parousia to its later association with His present exaltation find motivation for the shift in the

---

7. *The Titles of Jesus in Christology* (London, 1969), pp. 89ff.

delay of the parousia. But a large question mark should be set against the whole supposition that the delay in the parousia caused a major change in early Christian perspective. That it constituted a problem is plain; but some of the leaders of apostolic Christianity appear to have taken the problem in their stride, realizing that the "when" of the parousia was its least important feature. We can trace the progression of Paul's thought in this regard from the earliest to the latest of his undisputed writings. For him the realization increased as time went on that his death before the parousia was more probable than his survival until it took place; but, far from making him recast the main lines of his thought, this realization enabled him to explore and expound essential Paulinism at a deeper level than before.

In short, it seems impossible on the available evidence to accept the view that the association of Jesus' Lordship with His present exaltation and the idea of His exercising an intercessory ministry at God's right hand resulted from the delay in the parousia. Both are attested too early in the first Christian generation to be plausibly accounted for in this way.

The invocation *Mārānā-thā* ("Our Lord, come!"), which appears in the *Didachē* (10:6) as a eucharistic prayer, was in all probability used in the early Palestinian Aramaic-speaking communities in a eucharistic context; otherwise it would be hard to account for its appearance in such a context in a Greek church order. It cannot indeed be proved that its one New Testament occurrence (I Cor. 16:22) is, as Hans Lietzmann suggested,[8] part of a quotation from a liturgical sequence, thus:

Versicle: If any one does not love the Lord, let him be anathema.

Response: Mārānā-thā!

Versicle: The grace of the Lord Jesus be with you.

But the occurrence of the Greek form of the invocation at the end of the Apocalypse (Rev. 22:20) comes in such a responsive setting, and that in a book which in its language, and especially in its hymnody, has been manifestly influenced by Christian liturgical use. We may reflect, moreover, that the Apocalypse, although we have it in a Greek text, is not generally regarded as a notably Hellenistic work.

In any case, the invocation is most appropriate to a eucharistic setting. At the last supper Jesus looked forward to His reunion

---

8. *Mass and Lord's Supper* (Leiden, 1953ff.), p. 193.

with His disciples in the kingdom of God, and His instruction that they should break bread as His memorial charges them to anticipate, if not to hasten, His parousia. Paul, as we have suggested above, puts this idea in his own words when he says that the eating of the bread and drinking from the cup constitute a proclamation of the Lord's death till He comes (I Cor. 11:26).[9] In the eucharist the partition between now and then, between "already" and "not yet," between the disciples' present condition and the coming advent, wore very thin. As Jesus had made Himself known to the two at Emmaus in the breaking of bread, so the disciples continued to pray especially at the eucharist that they might now see Him in their midst.

But in what sense is Jesus called *mārana* in this Aramaic invocation? Certainly in much more than a courtesy sense. The Aramaic *mārē* ("Lord") is used as a divine title in both pagan and Jewish Aramaic, and in the Targum on Job from Cave 11 at Qumran (on Job 34:12) it is used as a rendering of *shadday* ("the Almighty") in parallelism with *'elāhā* ("God").[10] In a Christian eucharistic setting a connotation approaching divinity is implied: "Our Lord, come!" is the only adequate rendering. But if indeed the setting of the invocation is eucharistic, it is the eucharistic setting of the early Aramaic-speaking Palestinian church. Whatever difficulties scholars may find in the way of accepting this, they are trifling compared with the difficulties attending any other account of the matter—such as that the language is that of the bilingual Christian community in or around Syrian Antioch or Damascus, or that the invocation has the form of an oath sworn to God and is not addressed to Christ. *Mārana-thā* is a testimony to the place which the exalted and expected Christ had in the worship of the most primitive church.

The most impressive evidence of the superlative connotation which *kyrios* carried as a designation of Jesus is the free application to Jesus in the New Testament of Septuagint quotations referring to the God of Israel (where *kyrios* is the rendering of Yahweh). This practice is not confined to one author or to one school of thought, but it is particularly marked in Paul. For him the Old Testament "day of Yahweh" becomes not only "the day of the Lord (*kyrios*)" as in the Septuagint but also "the day of

---

9. See pp. 43f.

10. According to M. Black, the form *mārē* or *māran* is used with reference to God in the Aramaic fragments of I Enoch from Qumran Cave 4 ("The Christological Use of the Old Testament in the New Testament," *New Testament Studies* 18 [1971-72], p. 10).

Christ" or "the day of our Lord Jesus (Christ)." Similarly, the assurance of salvation to anyone who confesses Jesus as Lord, already quoted from Romans 10:9, is buttressed by the promise of Joel 2:32: "Whoever invokes the name of the Lord (Hebrew *Yahweh*) will be saved" (Rom. 10:13).

What could have led Paul and others to this line of Old Testament interpretation?

The influence of Psalm 110:1 has been adduced as a factor. The oracle cited in this verse constitutes, as we have seen, a primitive Christian *testimonium* for Jesus' exaltation at God's right hand, while the words introducing the oracle, "An oracle of Yahweh to my lord," constitute a *testimonium* for his right to the designation "Lord." For it seems to have been common ground to Jews and Christians in New Testament times that the oracle was addressed to the Davidic Messiah, and for those who believed Jesus to be the Messiah the words introducing the oracle implied that Jesus was Lord. Thus in Acts 2:34-36 they provide the basis for Peter's peroration affirming that God has made the crucified Jesus "both Lord and Messiah," while in Mark 12:35-37 they give rise to the question how the Messiah, who was *ex hypothesi* David's son, could be described by David as "my lord." But the Greek version of the introductory words could have exercised a still more far-reaching influence, for in it *kyrios* is used not only as the rendering of "lord" (Hebrew *'ādōn*) but also as the rendering of *Yahweh:* "The Lord (*kyrios*) said to my lord (*kyrios*)." Such a two-fold use of *kyrios* in the same clause could have facilitated the practice of ascribing to Jesus Old Testament passages where *kyrios* is the Greek counterpart to *Yahweh*. But if Septuagint usage facilitated the practice, it cannot fully account for it. So far as Psalm 110 is concerned, consideration must be given to the fact that the person whom the psalmist calls "my lord" is invited by the God of Israel, who is also the God of heaven, to sit at His right hand; whatever of subordination this implies, it implies at the same time exaltation—exaltation to be Lord of the universe as well as Lord of the believing community.

The ascription to a man of Old Testament passages relating to the God of Israel would be incredible on the part of any Jew, "Hebrew" or Hellenist, did we not have New Testament evidence for their early and pervasive ascription to Jesus. It can be accounted for only by the immediate impact which personal confrontation with Jesus—living, crucified, risen, and exalted —made on His followers. The verbal coincidence in the Greek

Bible of *kyrios* as the rendering of Yahweh and *kyrios* as the rendering of *'ādōn* would not have been sufficient in itself to make them take a course which they would normally have felt by instinct to be blasphemous. It was because of nothing but the personal impact of Jesus in their experience that language which they would have repudiated as blasphemous if applied to anyone else appeared to be the most natural language in the world when applied spontaneously to him.

Of all the Old Testament passages with Yahweh as subject which the New Testament refers to Jesus, none is more interesting than Philippians 2:9-11, at which we have already looked. I need not recapitulate here the arguments for regarding the passage to which these verses belong as pre-Pauline. If it is pre-Pauline (and I think it is), Paul makes it his own. The "name above every name" bestowed by God on Jesus is almost certainly *kyrios* in the sense of Yahweh, and the affirmation that "Jesus Christ is *kyrios*" means, practically, that Jesus Christ is Yahweh. The Old Testament passage here alluded to is Isaiah 45:23, where Yahweh, proclaiming "I am God, and there is no other," goes on: "By myself I have sworn, from my mouth has gone forth in righteousness a word that shall not return: 'To me every knee shall bow, every tongue shall swear'." We should note, moreover, that this comes from a section of Old Testament prophecy where the exclusive power and glory of Yahweh as the only God are repeatedly underlined. "I am Yahweh, and there is no other, beside me there is no God" (Isa. 45:5; cf. 44:6, 8; 45:21); "I, I am Yahweh, and beside me there is no saviour" (Isa. 43:11); "I am Yahweh, that is my name; my glory I give to no other" (Isa. 42:8).

But in this early Christian hymn, to be dated within the first Christian generation, the supreme name is bestowed on Jesus, the glory of the only God is shared with Jesus, and not diminished but enhanced in the process—for when every tongue confesses that Jesus Christ is Lord, this is done "to the glory of God the Father." No angel or man, it is implied, by any act or word, can exalt Jesus so highly as God has already done. Even so, the Jesus who has been thus highly exalted is the Jesus who endured the death of the cross—that is to say, He is identical with the *historical* Jesus.

9 781532 690129